Vegan Instant Pot Cookbook.

101 EASY AND HEALTHY VEGAN INSTANT POT RECIPES FOR YOUR PRESSURE COOKER

INSTANT POT VEGAN COOKBOOK | instant vegan meals

© Text Copyright 2019 – Arnold Smith

The content contained within this book may not be reproduced, duplicated or transmitted without direct written permission from the author or the publisher.

Under no circumstances will any blame or legal responsibility be held against the publisher, or author, for any damages, reparation, or monetary loss due to the information contained within this book. Either directly or indirectly.

Legal Notice:

This book is copyright protected. This book is only for personal use. You cannot amend, distribute, sell, use, quote or paraphrase any part, or the content within this book, without the consent of the author or publisher.

Disclaimer Notice:

Please note the information contained within this document is for educational and entertainment purposes only. All effort has been executed to present accurate, up to date, and reliable, complete information. No warranties of any kind are declared or implied. Readers acknowledge that the author is not engaging in the rendering of legal, financial, medical or professional advice. The content within this book has been derived from various sources. Please consult a licensed professional before attempting any techniques outlined in this book.

By reading this document, the reader agrees that under no circumstances is the author responsible for any losses, direct or indirect, which are incurred as a result of the use of information contained within this document, including, but not limited to, — errors, omissions, or inaccuracies.

CONTENTS

Introduction: 4

Vegan made easy. 5

Instant pot basics. 12

Pantry basics, sauces and dips. 20

Vegetarian Dinners You Can Make in an Instant Pot. 35

Vegan Instant pot vegan satisfying sides recipes. 55

Vegan Comfort food favourite. 76

Vegan lunch recipes by instant pot. 98

Vegan breakfast recipes by instant pot. 123

Vegan Soups, stews and curries by instant pot. 141

Vegan Dessert recipes. 167

Summary. 186

INTRODUCTION:

One unexpected benefit of exploring a plant-based diet is that it can inspire you to discover the joy of cooking. Most hobbies cost money, but learning how to cook will save you piles of cash. Doing your own cooking is much cheaper than eating at restaurants or buying frozen foods, plus you'll be eating fresher, tastier meals made with higher-quality ingredients.

This edition of our cookbook actually covers a lot and we've included newly discovered recipes that would serve you a kind of savoury that you've never had; both new and long existing vegans. You really don't have to miss anything because you're vegan, in fact, you are advantaged because these meals gives you the best nutritional benefits and keeps you much healthier.

VEGAN MADE EASY.

Whatever brought you as far as getting this cookbook, you've already taken the all-important first step on your vegan journey. There's an absolute, fantastic journey for you ahead as you journey to becoming a vegan. It's actually very easy, easier for some though, like every other transitional step in life, it takes a little bit of time, patience and the right guidance.

A vegan lifestyle is compatible with the highest levels of health and fitness, protects huge numbers of animals, and is a potent way to combat climate change. Plus, the food is insanely delicious and it becomes more widely available every year.

Keep your end goal in mind, but go at your own pace. Some people manage to go vegan overnight and if that's the right approach for you, fantastic. But don't be concerned if you feel you need more time. Like any other lifestyle change, going vegan not only takes getting used to, but it takes time to determine what will work best for you. It's not a one size fits all experience and there are numerous approaches you can take.

Making small changes to your everyday meals is one of the easiest ways to increase the amount of plant-based foods in your diet. You could start by removing meat or dairy one day a week and go from there. Or you could try changing one meal at a time, having vegan breakfasts during your first week, adding a vegan lunch during week two and so on. You could even try changing one product at a time by swapping cow's milk for almond or soya milk or butter for coconut oil or margarine. There's a plant-based alternative for almost every type of food you can think of, so you don't have to miss out on any of your favourite foods.

Make sure you don't miss out on essential nutrients. Just because you're vegan that doesn't mean you're 100% healthy, as there are vegan versions of almost every type of junk food you can think of. As long as you eat a wide variety of tasty plant foods, planning a healthy diet that incorporates all the vitamins and nutrients you need will be a breeze.

People commonly assume that going vegan requires enormous discipline and dedication. Luckily, nothing could be further from the truth. Switching to a vegan diet is surprisingly easy—and just a little reading puts you halfway there. Most new vegans end up being shocked by how little effort the transition takes.

Let's start by looking at how to construct a smart overall approach. The most obvious way to become vegan is to focus on eliminating animal products from your diet. Surprisingly, however, this method of transitioning is needlessly difficult. The truth is that gritting your teeth and exerting willpower makes the task of becoming vegan needlessly difficult. So let's look at a better way

Go Vegan by Crowding, Not Cutting— Instead of trying to cut animal products out of your diet, crowd them out. Constantly seek out new vegan foods. Every time you discover one you adore, it'll push the animal-based foods in your life further to the fringes. The more vegan foods you sample, the easier it becomes to eat vegan most of the time.

So cultivate the habit of trying new foods at every opportunity. The payoff is huge, and the commitment required is tiny. Just make a point of sampling at least five new vegan foods each week, and you'll discover a steady stream of foods you love. Week by week, these items will begin crowding out the animal products that are currently in your diet. Before long, anytime you get hungry the first food that comes to mind will be vegan.

You'll Find a Vast Assortment of Delicious Vegan Foods— Does going vegan mean you'll need to spend loads of time in the kitchen? Absolutely not. You'll be amazed by how many instant and near-instant options exist. THIS COOKBOOK is a large step in the right direction to soothing that.

How Fast Should You Go?— Since a key part of learning how to go vegan involves discovering new foods, you're always in control of how fast or slow you go. You certainly don't need to go vegan all at once. Some people do it overnight, while others ease into it over months or even years. How fast you go is not nearly as important as whether the approach you take feels easy and comfortable. Use whatever stepping-stones work for you. The goal, after all, is not just to go vegan but to stay vegan long-term. You want fill your diet with delicious vegan foods that you're delighted to eat every day.

Dipping in Your Toe— some people get intimidated by the thought of becoming absolutely, positively vegan—with no room for slips or exceptions. If making a 100 percent commitment sounds too much for you right now, no problem. There are always smaller steps that still accomplish a great deal of good.

One of America's most influential food writers, Mark Bittman, has long followed what he calls a "Vegan before 6:00," approach. That is, he follows a totally vegan diet from morning through afternoon, and then eats whatever he likes for dinner and the rest of the evening. Bittman's approach can easily get you past the halfway point towards becoming vegan. Simply by following Vegan before 6:00, you'll doubtless eat far fewer animal products than most people. If this approach sounds appealing, you can get hold of Bittman's book on the topic.

Buying Vegan Foods Online— If you live in a community that lacks a good natural foods store, don't despair. Amazon.com can pick up the slack. They carry all sorts of essential vegan items, from energy bars to hot cereals to cookies to nutritional yeast. You can find every imaginable vegan food product on Amazon.com. The trouble is that many items listed by third parties sell for exorbitant prices. But Amazon itself fulfils dozens of great vegan foods, at prices that are remarkably competitive.

We maintain a grocery page listing Amazon's best vegan food deals. It's worth checking out even if you have a good natural foods store nearby, since you will certainly find items unavailable locally. Amazon won't carry every vegan grocery item you need, but you can save a lot of time and money by ordering some of your groceries through them.

INSTANT POT BASICS.

The Instant Pot isn't nearly as simple or "instant" as you might think it is. In fact, they are pretty complicated and many folks never use half of the functions available.

What is the Instant Pot?

It is one appliance that has many functions: electric pressure cooker, rice cooker, steamer, yogurt maker, sauté pan, slow cooker and warmer. The function that most people praise the Instant Pot for is the electric pressure cooker feature, but I personally LOVE its slow cooker feature.

Are electric pressure cookers safe?

Yes and no. They still have a danger factor, but knowing how to use yours will prevent injury. The Instant Pot has a safety feature of locking until the pressure is released an safe to open so there is no guessing. However, the "quick release" function, also known as "venting" or QR, releases some pretty hot steam that could easily cause harm or injury. Your Instant Pot is locked when the little metal piece right next to the valve is UP.

Do I need to use liquid?

Yes, by definition, pressure cookers need some amount of liquid to build pressure. You need at least 1/2 cup to 1 cup of liquid for your Instant Pot to work. For dry foods, more is needed, but if you are using water containing foods, like vegetables, less is needed.

What can I make in the Instant Pot?

Most people think of fried chicken when they think of electric pressure cookers, but you can make so many things. Chuck roasts will be fork tender, chicken will shred in just 10 minutes and seafood will be done in 4 minutes. You can also make desserts, such as cakes and puddings, cheese, yogurt, broths, stocks and stubborn grains like quinoa, sorghum and steel cut oats in just minutes.

Why isn't the timer starting right away on my Instant Pot?

I think one of the things that frustrates me the most about recipe writers for the Instant Pot, they never include the amount of time it takes for the pot to build pressure or heat. If you are starting with cold or frozen foods, it will take longer to come to pressure (see what this means below), whereas hot or previously simmered/sautéed foods won't take as long. Plan for anywhere between 10-15 minutes additional time for the Instant Pot to come to pressure.

What is NPR or natural pressure release?

Natural pressure release is sometimes abbreviated to NP or NPR. It basically means you are going to gradually (and naturally) allow the pressure to release. This process takes about 15-20 minutes. Food will continue to cook while on natural pressure release.

What is QR or quick pressure release?

It is the opposite of NPR. Instead of allowing the pressure to gradually release, you vent it out super-fast. Be careful though, this steam is HOT and can cause injury. Also, don't do it under your cabinets or around anything that has a painted finish- it will literally peel the paint. Release pressure in an open space on the counter.

What is venting and sealing?

The knob on the Instant Pot has two settings: venting and sealing. Venting means that you are not building up pressure at all, instead the pressure and steam is releasing during the cooking process. This is used for steaming. Sealing means that you are pressure cooking and all of that good stuff is staying inside the Instant Pot.

What is PIP?

PIP stands for "pot in pot" cooking. Basically, another pot that goes into the inner pot. You need this for casseroles, cakes and if you want to cook multiple things at once. The Instant makes some fabulous cheesecakes! These are the ones I use the most:

- 1 quart casserole dish
- 7 inch spring form pan
- Steamer basket.

Do I still need a slow cooker if I have an Instant Pot?

Technically, no, the Instant Pot is also a slow cooker. One of the things I love about the Instant Pot as a slow cooker is that I can use the Sauté function either before slow cooking to brown the meat or at the very end to reduce or thicken sauces, eliminating the need to use even more dishes.

How do I use the trivet?

The trivet can be used in multiple ways. Put the "legs" down and you can cook two things at once- meat on the and set the steam basket on top or vice versa or... put the "legs" up and now you can use them as handles to pull out things like the spring form pan.

Why does my Instant Pot smell?

It is most likely due to the silicone sealing ring. This ring holds in smells like no other. You can buy extras and use one for savoury dishes and another for sweet meals. I have one I use just for curry. Also, make sure to rinse the lid of the Instant Pot to get out smells. Many folks wash the inner pot, but not the lid! The rings are cheap.

What is the difference between low and high pressure?

The quick and dirty answer is that high pressure is better for cooking heartier items, like meats, chicken and pasta, while low pressure is better suited for delicate items like eggs, fish and some desserts. Why? First understand PSI, pounds per square inch. The PSI determines just how hot the cooker is going to get beyond the regular 212 Fahrenheit temperature, the boiling point of water at sea level.

A high pressure could get up to 10 or 12 PSI and as hot as 239 to 245 Fahrenheit, while a low pressure setting is between 5.5 to 7 PSI, with a temperature range from 229 to 233 Fahrenheit. Low pressure items might need to cook longer, but will benefit in the texture from lower pressure.

How do I use the Instant Pot at high altitude?

Some say that a pressure cooker defies nature and that altitude doesn't matter, but anyone who lives in a high altitude area (3,000 feet above sea level) will tell you that isn't true. According to the New High Altitude Cookbook, cooking time under pressure should be increased by 5% for every 1,000 feet after 2,000 feet above sea level.

Is it necessary to do the Water Test?

Yes! To make sure your Instant Pot is safe and comes to correct temperatures for cooking, do the water test. It really doesn't take long.

PANTRY BASICS, SAUCES AND DIPS.

Spaghetti Sauce: This rich and tasty homemade spaghetti sauce is made with fresh tomatoes! Just what you need for any pasta dish, and so quick and easy to make in the Instant Pot.

Ingredient: 2 tablespoons olive oil, 2 yellow onions, chopped, 2 cloves garlic, minced. 1 carrot, chopped. 1 celery stalk, chopped. 3 pounds plum tomatoes, 1 teaspoon dried oregano, 1 teaspoon Italian seasoning, 1 teaspoon sea salt, 1 teaspoon dried basil, 1/2 teaspoon ground black pepper.

Preparation: Turn on a multi-functional pressure cooker (such as Instant Pot(R)) and select Sauté function. Heat olive oil and stir in onions and garlic; cook until soft and translucent, about 5 minutes. Add carrot, celery, and tomatoes; cook until tender, about 4 minutes. Season with oregano, Italian seasoning, salt, basil, and pepper. Close and lock the lid. Select high pressure according to manufacturer's instructions; set timer for 25 minutes. Allow 10 to 15 minutes for pressure to build.

Release pressure using the natural-release method according to manufacturer's instructions, 10 to 40 minutes. Unlock and remove the lid. Blend with an immersion blender to desired consistency.

Instant Pot Vegan Cheese Sauce: This vegan cheese sauce recipe is so simple to make in the Instant Pot. You just need to dump everything together, cook it on high pressure and then puree it in a blender to a smooth sauce. So easy and tasty!

Ingredient: 1 large russet potato, 320 grams, cubed, 1 large sweet potato, 300 grams, cubed 2 large carrots, 170 grams, cut into rounds, 1/4 cup cashews, raw, 35 grams, 1 cup water, 8 oz., 1/2 cup nutritional yeast, 3/4 teaspoon smoked paprika, 1 teaspoon garlic powder. 1.25 teaspoon salt, or to taste, 1/4 teaspoon turmeric powder, 1 tablespoon white vinegar, 1.5 tablespoons lemon juice, 1/4 cup water or almond milk, 2 oz.

Preparation: To your instant pot add cubed potatoes, sweet potatoes, carrots, cashews and 1 cup water. Close the pot with its lid. Press the manual/pressure cook button and cook on high pressure for 5 minutes. The pressure valve should be in the sealing position. Let the pressure release naturally for 5 minutes and then do a quick pressure release by manually moving the valve from sealing to venting position. Let the veggies cool down a bit and then transfer them to a high speed blender. Add nutritional yeast, smoked paprika, garlic powder, salt, turmeric, white vinegar, lemon juice and 1/4 cup of either water or almond milk.

Pulse for 30 seconds or until the sauce is super creamy and smooth. Transfer vegan cheese sauce to serving bowl. Enjoy with chips or veggies!

Vegan Cheese Sauce: what truly makes this THE BEST Vegan Cheese Sauce Ever, is how quick and simple it is to make! Just throw all the ingredients into the INSTANT POT and in about 20 minutes you'll have a hot, delicious plant-based CHEESE SAUCE! Now how easy is that!

Ingredient: 2 cups water, 1/2 yellow or white onion, peeled and quartered, 2 cloves garlic, peeled, 1 cup carrots, peeled and sliced, 1 & 1/2 cups peeled and chopped Yukon Gold potatoes, 1/2 cup raw cashews (optional, but recommended for maximum creaminess.), 1/2 cup nutritional yeast (Different from baking yeast), 2 Tablespoons mellow white miso, 1 teaspoon smoked or sweet paprika, 1 1/2 Tablespoons lemon juice, 1 1/2 Tablespoons apple cider vinegar, 2 teaspoons sea salt (optional, but recommended to achieve a true cheese-like taste.)

Preparation: Place all ingredients in the Instant Pot in the order listed. (No need to soak the cashews- the Instant Pot will soften them.) Put the lid on the Instant Pot and twist it to the lock position. Select MANUAL with

HIGH pressure, then set the cook time to 5 MINUTES. While the cheese sauce is coming up to pressure and cooking in the Instant Pot, prepare the food you would like to serve with it, such as elbow macaroni, broccoli, baked potatoes, tortilla chips, etc. When the Instant Pot has finished cooking, manually release the pressure and open the lid.

Using hot pads and avoiding the steam, lift the stainless steel pot out of the cooker. Carefully pour the entire contents of the pot into a high speed blender. Puree using the whole juice setting, or use the highest speed setting for about 2 minutes, until sauce is super smooth, thick and creamy. (If sauce is too thick, add 1/4 to 1/2 cup plant milk and blend again to thin. Sauce will continue to thicken as it cools, so you may want to make it a little thinner to start.) Alternately, you can use a hand-held immersion blender directly in the Instant Pot to blend all ingredients together for 2-3 minutes, or until cheese sauce is super smooth, thinning with a little additional plant milk as needed. Serve hot cheese sauce immediately by pouring over cooked macaroni, steamed broccoli, baked potatoes, or stir in spices and serve over baked corn tortilla chips as nachos.

If not serving right away, allow cheese sauce to cool completely and then store covered in the refrigerator for up to one week, or in the freezer for up to three months. (Sauce will thicken when chilled, so you may need to thin it down again before serving, by adding a bit of plant milk or water while re-heating) When ready to serve the previously refrigerated or frozen sauce, heat in the microwave till super-hot, stirring every 2-3 minutes.

Continue heating and stirring until all the cold clumps have melted, and the sauce once again has a super smooth consistency.) Alternately, you can heat the thawed sauce in a saucepan on the stovetop, stirring constantly, until very hot and no lumps remain, and thinning with a bit of plant milk as needed (The heating process will thicken the sauce, so you may need to add even more plant milk to thin it out again before serving.)

Penne in Cajun Mustard Cream Sauce: Make this Instant Pot Penne in Cajun Mustard Cream Sauce for a quick and easy weeknight meal. With options to prepare it with Andouille sausage or meatless you can make everyone happy.

Ingredient: 12 ounces penne rigate pasta, uncooked, 2 1/2 cups chicken broth (for more flavour) or water, 2–3 tsp. Cajun seasoning, 1 tsp. garlic powder, 1 Tbsp. butter, 1 (14.5 oz.) can petite diced tomatoes, 1 (13 oz.) package Cajun-style Andouille smoked sausage (optional), 4 oz. cream cheese, 1 Tbsp. lemon juice, 1 1/2 tsp. Dijon mustard.

Preparation: Add pasta to the Instant Pot. Pour broth/water over the top, try to cover pasta as much as possible. Sprinkle in 2 tsp. of the Cajun seasoning and add in the garlic powder. Add in the butter and petite diced tomatoes. If using sausage, slice it into 1/2 inch pieces and add it into the pot. Cover the pot and secure the lid. Make sure valve is set to sealing. Set the manual/pressure cook button to 5 minutes. When time is up move valve to venting for a quick release (you can also use a natural pressure release).

Turn the pot to the sauté setting and stir in the cream cheese, until it is melted. Turn off the sauté setting. Stir in the lemon juice and Dijon mustard. Taste and if needed add in another teaspoon of Cajun seasoning. Salt and pepper to taste as needed.

Serve and enjoy. Store leftovers in an airtight container in the refrigerator for up to 3 days.

Easy Instant Pot Spaghetti Sauce: Easy Instant Pot Spaghetti Sauce–this spaghetti sauce is so delicious you'll be licking your plate. The funny part is that it only takes a handful of easy ingredients and a few minutes in your pressure cooker. Bonus–if you want to cook a spaghetti squash at the same time as the sauce you can!

Ingredient: 1 (28 oz.) can crushed tomatoes, 4 Tbsp. butter, 1 tsp. onion powder, 1 tsp. garlic powder, 1/2 tsp. kosher salt, Optional: 1 small spaghetti squash.

Preparation: Add tomatoes, butter, onion powder, garlic powder and salt to Instant Pot.

Optional: If making a spaghetti squash, use a paring knife to cut your spaghetti squash in half crosswise (not lengthwise). Use a spoon to scoop out all the seeds and gunk. Place a trivet inside the pot and then arrange the 2 squash halves to fit in the pot. Cover the pot and secure the lid. Make sure valve is set to sealing. Set the manual/pressure cook button to 7 minutes. Once the time has counted down and the pot beeps you can perform a quick release by moving the valve to venting. Remove the lid. Use tongs to remove the squash to a cutting board. Once it has cooled, use a fork to shred the flesh of the squash into long spaghetti-like strands. Use an immersion blender to blend the sauce to desired consistency. Salt and pepper the sauce to taste.

Serve the sauce over spaghetti or spaghetti squash and top with generous amounts of parmesan cheese.

Instant-Pot Vegan Cauliflower Queso: Cauliflower is a magical vegetable. It's tasty on its own, but it can transform into oil-free creamy sauces and even replace meat. In this recipe, it's the base for my favourite creamy, cheesy queso sauce. This is great on chips but even better on top of burritos and enchiladas. Best of all, you can get the pickiest of eaters to eat their veggies this way.

Ingredient: 2 cups (214 g) cauliflower florets (about 1/2 head small cauliflower), 1 cup (237 ml) water, 3/4 cup (96 g) thick-cut carrot coins, 1/4 cup (34 g) raw cashews, 1/4 cup (24 g) nutritional yeast, Liquid drained from 1 (10-oz [283-g]) can diced tomatoes with green chillies (I like Rotel), 1/2 tsp. smoked paprika, 1/2 tsp. salt (or to taste), 1/4 tsp. chili powder, 1/4 tsp. jalapeño powder, optional, 1/8 tsp. mustard powder.

Preparation: For the Instant Pot, add the cauliflower, water, carrots and cashews to your Instant Pot and cook on high pressure for 5 minutes, then carefully do a quick pressure release by moving the valve to release the pressure.

Pour the cooked mixture into a strainer over the sink and drain the extra water.

For the blender, put the drained mixture along with the nutritional yeast, liquid drained from the canned tomatoes, smoked paprika, salt, chili powder, jalapeño powder (if using) and mustard powder into your blender. Blend until smooth.

For the mix-ins, scrape out the blender contents into a mixing bowl and stir in the tomatoes and green chillies, bell pepper (if using), minced onion (if using) and cilantro.

You can serve this at room temperature or keep it warm on the lowest slow cooker setting.

INSTANT POT BLACK BEAN DIP: Instant Pot Black Bean Dip is a total breeze to throw together! No cans needed! Simply grab a bag of dried beans and get ready for a party-perfect vegetarian dip that's easy, make-ahead, and SO delicious!

Ingredient: 1.5 cups dried black beans, 1 medium onion, diced, 4 cloves garlic, peeled + minced, 2 medium jalapeños (approx. 1/3 cup chopped), 14.5 oz. can diced or crushed tomatoes, 1 + 3/4 cup vegetable broth, 1.5 TBSP avocado oil, juice of 1 lime, 2 tsp. ground cumin, 1 tsp. smoked paprika, 3/4 tsp. sea salt, 1/2 tsp. chili powder, 1/2 tsp. ground coriander, 4 ounces softened cream cheese, 1 cup freshly grated pepper jack and/or cheddar cheese, chopped tomatoes, sliced jalapeños, diced bell pepper, chopped red onion, cilantro, sour cream, Greek yogurt, salsa, Pico de Gallo, guacamole.

Preparation: Rinse your black beans and toss them in your Instant Pot. Dice and chop your veggies and mince your garlic. Add veggies, garlic, tomatoes, broth, oil, lime juice, and spices to the pot and mix. Press the bean button and cook for 30 minutes high pressure. Allow a natural release (NR) for 10 minutes then quick release (QR) remaining pressure. Use an immersion blender (or a blender or food processor) to blend the tip into creamy deliciousness and once cooled slightly, give it a taste. You can adjust the spiciness by adding anything from hot sauce, spicy salsa, red pepper flakes, or cayenne to the mix and add any extra spices/salt to suit your tastes. As written, it's on the mild side. Serve piled high with all your favourite toppings and dig in!

VEGETARIAN DINNERS YOU CAN MAKE IN AN INSTANT POT.

The Instant Pot is awesome at cooking some of our favourite vegetarian staples, from perfectly cooked dried beans to tender, well-seasoned spaghetti squash. But it can just as easily deliver complete weeknight dinners. Here are 10 vegetarian dinner recipes using both the pressure cooker and slow cooker functions of your Instant Pot, proving it isn't just for basics.

Instant Pot sweet potatoes: If you've never made an Instant Pot sweet potato, are you in for a treat! Thanks to the Instant Pot, you won't have to wait over an hour for sweet potatoes to bake in the oven.

Ingredients: 1 cup water, 4 sweet potatoes (should be between 3-4 inches in diameter)

Topping ideas: Black beans, Corn, Pico de Gallo, Cilantro, Jalapeno peppers, Green onions, Red onion, Sautéed bell peppers, Sour cream, Shredded cheese.

Preparation: Add 1 cup of water to Instant Pot. Add trivet, then add sweet potatoes. Place lid on Instant Pot and make sure valve is set to seal. Press the pressure cook button and set to high, then cook for 15 minutes. Instant Pot will take about 10 minutes to come to pressure then pressure cook the 15 minutes.

Allow the pressure to release naturally (about 10-15 minutes), then open the lid when pressure gauge has dropped and the lid opens easily. Let cool about 5-10 minutes, then remove sweet potatoes and slice in half. Load with toppings of choice, adding the cheese first if using to ensure it melts. Serve and enjoy! Sweet potato leftovers can be refrigerated up to 5 days.

To freeze sweet potatoes: wrap in foil once cooled for 30-40 min and freeze up to 3 months. Reheat in the microwave for 7-8 minutes to defrost and serve.

PORTOBELLO POT ROAST: This hearty pot roast has all the savoury flavours of a beefy dish, but without the beef. Using the Instant Pot's slow-cook function gives the flavours plenty of time to meld.

Ingredient: 1.25 pounds Yukon gold potatoes, cut into bite-sized pieces, 1 pound baby belle mushrooms (if they are large, cut them in half), 2 large carrots, peeled and cut into bite-sized pieces, 2 cups frozen pearl onions, 4 cloves garlic, peeled and minced, 3 sprigs fresh thyme, 3, cups vegetable stock, divided, 1/2 cup dry red or white wine, 3 tablespoons tomato paste, 2 tablespoons vegetarian Worcestershire sauce, 2 tablespoons corn-starch, Kosher salt and freshly-cracked black pepper, Optional garnish: finely-chopped fresh parsley.

Preparation: Add potatoes, mushrooms, carrots, onions, garlic, thyme, 2.5 cups vegetable stock, wine and Worcestershire together in the bowl of a pressure cooker, and gently toss to combine. Close lid securely and set vent to "Sealing". Press "Manual", then press "Pressure" until the light on "High

Pressure" lights up, then adjust the up/down arrows until time reads 20 minutes. Cook. Then let the pressure release naturally, about 15 minutes. Carefully turn the vent to "Venting", just to release any extra pressure that might still be in there. Remove the lid.

In a separate bowl, whisk together the remaining 1/2 cup vegetable stock and corn-starch until combined. Add to the roast mixture, and gently toss to combine. Continue to cook for 1-3 minutes, until the sauce thickens up a bit.

Serve immediately, garnished with fresh parsley if desired.

Note: be sure to use vegan Worcestershire sauce.

Instant Pot Minestrone: Here, Instant Pot basics like beans and broth come together to make a wondrous version of the soup we all know and love: minestrone!

Ingredient: 2 tablespoons olive oil, 3 cloves garlic, minced, 1 onion, diced, 2 carrots, peeled and diced, 2 stalks celery, diced, 1 1/2 teaspoons dried basil, 1 teaspoon dried oregano, 1/2 teaspoon fennel seed, 6 cups low sodium chicken broth, 1 (28-ounce) can diced tomatoes, 1 (16-ounce) can kidney beans, drained and rinsed, 1 zucchini, chopped, 1 (3-inch) Parmesan rind, 1 bay leaf, 1 bunch kale, stems removed and leaves chopped, 2 teaspoons red wine vinegar, Kosher salt and freshly ground black pepper, to taste, 1/3 cup freshly grated Parmesan, 2 tablespoons chopped fresh parsley leaves.

Preparation: Set a 6-qt Instant Pot to the high sauté setting. Add olive oil, garlic, onion, carrots and celery. Cook, stirring occasionally, until tender, about 2-3 minutes. Stir in basil, oregano and fennel seed until fragrant, about 1 minute. Stir in chicken stock, diced tomatoes, kidney beans, zucchini, Parmesan rind and bay leaf. Select manual setting; adjust pressure to high, and set time for 5 minutes. When finished cooking, quick-release pressure according to manufacturer's directions. Stir in kale until wilted, about 2 minutes. Stir in red wine vinegar; season with salt and pepper, to taste.

Serve immediately, garnished with Parmesan and parsley, if desired.

Ethiopian-Style Spinach & Lentil Soup: This simple-looking lentil soup comes together quickly and is packed with warm spices and bright, lemony flavour.

Ingredient: 2 tablespoons unsalted butter, 1 tablespoon olive oil, 1 medium red onion, finely chopped, 1 teaspoon garlic powder, 2 teaspoons ground coriander, 1/2 teaspoon cinnamon powder, 1/2 teaspoon turmeric powder, 1/4 teaspoon clove powder, 1/4 teaspoon cayenne pepper, 1/4 teaspoon cardamom powder, 1/4 teaspoon fresh grated nutmeg, 2 cups brown lentils, 8 cups water, 2 teaspoons salt, 1/4 teaspoon pepper, 6 ounces fresh spinach or baby spinach (about 4 packed cups), 4 tablespoons lemon juice.

Preparation: Preheat the pressure cooker (by pressing brown/sauté mode). Add the butter, oil, onion, garlic, coriander, cinnamon, turmeric, clove, cayenne, cardamom, and nutmeg. Sauté three minutes. Add the lentils and water. Close the lid and pressure-cook for 10 minutes at high pressure. When time is up, open the pressure cooker with natural release: Turn off the pressure cooker and wait for pressure to come down naturally, about 15 to 20 minutes.

Remove the lid, tilting it away from you. Add the salt and pepper, and mix in the spinach leaves to wilt them into the soup.

Stir in the fresh lemon juice and serve.

Chana Masala: Chana masala — dried chickpeas slow-cooked with tomatoes and spices — is one of those dinners that an Instant Pot or other slow cooker excels at. Assemble it in the morning and come home to a comforting dinner that will have everyone asking for seconds.

Ingredient: 2 cups dried chickpeas, 5 to 6 1/2 cups hot water, depending on desired consistency, 2 black cardamom pods, 2 (1-inch) pieces cassia, 4 to 6 cloves, 2 bay leaves, 1/4 teaspoon turmeric, 1/4 teaspoon ground Indian red chili, 1 1/2 to 2 teaspoon salt

For the masala: 3 tablespoons canola oil, 1 large yellow onion, diced small, 6 cloves garlic, coarsely chopped, 1 (2-inch) piece fresh ginger, peeled and coarsely chopped, about 1 tablespoon, 3 whole peeled tomatoes (canned or fresh) or 8 ounces diced canned tomatoes, 1 1/2 tablespoons ground coriander, 2 teaspoons ground cumin, 1/4 teaspoon turmeric, 1/4 teaspoon ground Indian red chili, 3/4 teaspoon green mango powder, 1/2 teaspoon black salt, 1/2 teaspoon ground black pepper, 2 Serrano chillies, halved lengthwise, 1/4 cup water, Chopped cilantro, for garnish.

Instant Pot Potato and Corn Chowder: Potato and corn chowder is a family favourite. Just make sure to use veggie stock instead of chicken, and of course skip the bacon. And since the Instant Pot does all the work here, don't skimp on the toppings.

Ingredient: 2 slices thick cut bacon chopped, 1/2 medium onion finely chopped, 1 rib celery finely chopped, 1 teaspoon minced garlic, 1 teaspoon salt, 1/4 teaspoon dried thyme, 1/8 teaspoon black pepper, 2 1/2 cups low sodium chicken broth, 3/4 pound Little potatoes any varietal (about 15 potatoes), 4 ears corn, 1/2 cup half and half cream, 1 tablespoon corn starch, shredded cheese or green onions for garnish.

Preparation: Turn the Instant Pot (mine is a 6 quart) to sauté. Add the bacon and onions and cook for 3-4 minutes until browned. Add the celery, garlic, salt, thyme and pepper and cook and stir 1 minute. Add the broth and scrape any browned bits off of the bottom (this helps to prevent a burn message and adds lots of flavour). Turn off the Instant Pot. Roughly chop the little potatoes. Use a knife to remove the corn kernels from the ears. Add potatoes and corn to the Instant Pot. Put the lid on, turn the valve to sealing, and select Manual or Pressure Cook for 2 minutes. It will take about 10-15 minutes to come to pressure and begin counting down. When the cook time is over, let the pressure release naturally for a few minutes, and then open the valve to release remaining pressure. Turn the Instant Pot to sauté, whisk together cream and corn starch and stir into soup to thicken slightly.

Serve with shredded cheese and green onions as desired.

Chickpea Tomato Soup: This Chickpea Tomato Soup is an easy, hearty soup, loaded with chickpeas and vegetables in every bite.

Ingredient: 1 tsp. olive oil, 1/2 cup chopped onion, 1/2 cup diced carrots, 1/2 cup diced celery, 2 garlic cloves, minced, 2 15 oz. cans chickpeas, rinsed and drained, 1 28 oz. can crushed tomatoes, 3 cups reduced sodium chicken broth, or vegetable broth for vegetarians, 1 fresh rosemary sprig, 2 bay leaves, 2 tbsp. chopped fresh basil, fresh black pepper, to taste, 2 cups fresh baby spinach, 1/4 cup shredded parmesan cheese, plus extra optional for garnish.

Preparation: Heat oil in a large non-stick skillet over medium heat. Add the carrots, celery, onion, garlic and sauté until tender and fragrant, about 6 to 8 minutes. Transfer to the instant pot along with the broth, tomatoes, chickpeas, parmesan cheese, and pepper. Add the rosemary, bay leaves and basil, cover and cook on low for 6 hours. When done add the spinach. Remove bay leaves, rosemary sprig and season to taste with salt and black pepper. Ladle soup into bowls and top with extra parmesan cheese if desired.

Slow Cooker Baked Ziti: If you haven't already discovered the pleasure of slow-cooking baked pasta, let me introduce you via the Instant Pot. This cheesy baked ziti is a hit with the whole family.

Ingredient: Cooking spray, 1 pound dried ziti pasta, 48 ounces marinara sauce, 1 (15-ounce) container whole milk ricotta cheese, 2 cups shredded low-moisture mozzarella cheese, divided.

Preparation: Coat a 6-quart or larger slow cooker with cooking spray. Add the ziti, marinara, ricotta, and 1 cup of the mozzarella cheese, and stir well to combine. Sprinkle with the remaining 1 cup of mozzarella.

Cover and cook until the pasta is cooked through and the cheese is melted, on the LOW setting for 3 to 4 hours or on the HIGH setting for 1 to 2 hours. Serve immediately.

Creamy Instant Pot Pasta: This recipe is a seriously creamy Instant Pot pasta recipe that you'll make again and again.

Ingredient: 1 1/2 cups water, 28 ounce can crushed fire roasted tomatoes (or best quality crushed tomatoes), 2 tablespoons olive oil, 1 tablespoon balsamic vinegar, 2 teaspoons garlic powder, 1 teaspoon dried oregano, 1 teaspoon kosher salt, 2 cups baby spinach leaves, tightly packed (or chopped spinach), 8 fresh basil leaves, 8 ounces penne pasta (regular, not whole wheat), 4 ounce goat cheese log

Preparation: Place the following ingredients into the Instant Pot: water, tomatoes, olive oil, balsamic vinegar, garlic powder, oregano, kosher salt, spinach, whole basil leaves, and penne. Cook on high pressure for 5 minutes: Press the Pressure Cook button, making sure the "High Pressure" setting is selected, and set the time. Note that it takes about 10 minutes for the pot to "preheat" and come up to pressure before it starts cooking. (During cooking, avoid touching the metal part of the lid.)

Quick release: Vent the remaining steam from the Instant Pot by moving the pressure release handle to "Venting", covering your hand with a towel or hot pad. Never put your hands or face near the vent when releasing steam. Open the pressure cooker lid.

Open the lid and crumble in the goat cheese; stir until a creamy sauce forms. The sauce will thicken even more as it cools.

Instant Pot Acorn Squash: This vegetarian stuffed acorn squash features a rice stuffing with toasted pecans.

Ingredient: 1 cup white basmati rice, 1/2 teaspoon dried sage, 1/2 teaspoon kosher salt, divided, plus more for sprinkling, 2 small acorn squash, 1 small yellow onion, 2 cloves garlic, 2 stalks celery, 1 tablespoon olive oil, plus more for drizzling, 1 teaspoon dried thyme, 1 teaspoon dried oregano, Fresh ground black pepper, 3 tablespoons unsalted butter, 3/4 cup raw pecan pieces, Feta or goat cheese crumbles, optional.

Preparation: Cook the rice: In an Instant Pot or digital pressure cooker, stir the rice, sage, 1/4 teaspoon kosher salt, and 1 cup of water. Pressure cook on high for 3 minutes. Then vent any remaining steam by moving the pressure release handle to "Venting", covering your hand with a towel or hot pad. (Never put your hands or face near the steam release valve when releasing steam.)

Prep the veggies: While the rice cooks, cut the squash in half and remove seeds, then cut it in half again (into quarters). Dice the onion and celery. Mince the garlic.

Toast the pecans: In a dry skillet over low heat, toast the pecans for about 3 minutes, stirring occasionally, until fragrant. Make the stuffing: Heat the olive oil in a skillet over medium heat. Sauté the onion and celery 5 to 7 minutes until tender and translucent. Add the garlic, thyme, and oregano, and sauté for an additional 2 minutes until fragrant. When the rice is cooked, stir it into the skillet. Stir in 1/4 teaspoon kosher salt, the fresh ground black pepper, butter, and pecans.

Cook the squash: Rinse the Instant Pot and place the steamer basket in the bottom with 1 cup of water. Rub the squash quarters with a bit of olive oil and sprinkle with a few pinches of dried oregano. Place the squash quarters in the pot, stacking as necessary. Pressure cook on high for 6 minutes. After the pot beeps, immediately do a Quick Release: vent the remaining steam by moving the pressure release handle to "Venting", covering your hand with a towel or hot pad.

Serve: Carefully remove the squash from the Instant Pot and sprinkle it with kosher salt. Spoon the stuffing over the squash quarters and serve immediately.

INSTANT POT VEGAN SATISFYING SIDES RECIPES.

Instant Pot 3-Cheese Macaroni and Cheese: This mac and cheese is decadent and over the top delicious. It makes a whole lot and is perfect to bring to a potluck or to serve a crowd.

Ingredient: 3 ¾ cups water, 16 oz. uncooked macaroni noodles, 3 Tbsp. butter, 2 tsp. kosher salt, ½ tsp. pepper, 2 tsp. ground mustard, 1 cup whole milk or half and half, 8 ounces grated sharp cheddar, 8 ounces grated Monterey jack cheese, 8 ounces grated Colby jack cheese, 1 cup panko breadcrumbs (optional).

Preparation: Pour the water into the Instant Pot. Add in the macaroni, butter, salt, pepper and ground mustard. Cover and secure the lid. Make sure the valve is set to sealing. Set the manual/pressure cook button to 4 minutes on high pressure. When the time is up let the pot sit for 5 minutes and then move the valve to venting. Remove the lid and stir in the milk. Then stir in the cheeses a couple of cups at a time until all the cheese is stirred in and creamy and smooth. Optional breadcrumb topping: Unplug your Instant Pot. Sprinkle the breadcrumbs on top of the macaroni and cheese. Place your Crisp Lid on top of the pot. Click the lid into place and set the temperature to 500 degrees and the timer to 4 minutes. When the time is up remove the lid and serve the mac and cheese. If you don't have a Crisp Lid then you can scoop the mac and cheese into a 9×13 inch pan. Sprinkle the breadcrumbs on top and broil in your oven until the breadcrumbs are toasted.

Instant Pot Tomato Basil Parmesan Rice: creamy rice with a punch of flavour from cherry tomatoes and fresh basil. This rice is made quickly in your electric pressure cooker and is a great summer dinner or side dish.

Ingredient: 1 Tbsp. olive oil, ½ cup diced onion, 1 Tbsp. minced garlic, 1 ¾ cups chicken broth or veggie broth, 1 ½ cups uncooked brown rice, 1 (8 oz.) can tomato sauce, 2 cups halved cherry tomatoes, ¼ cup chopped fresh basil, 1 cup shredded or grated parmesan cheese, Salt and pepper.

Preparation: Turn your Instant Pot to the sauté setting. When the display says HOT add in the oil and swirl it around. Add in the onion and sauté for 4 minutes. Add in the garlic and sauté for 20 seconds. Add in the broth and scrape the bottom of the pot. Add in the rice. Then dump the tomato sauce on top without stirring. Cover the pot and secure the lid. Make sure valve is set to sealing.

Set the manual/pressure cook button to 22 minutes. When the time is up let the pot sit for 10 minutes and then move the valve to venting. Remove the lid.

Stir in the tomatoes, basil and parmesan cheese. Salt and pepper to taste. Serve.

Instant Pot Spaghetti Squash Mac and Cheese: if you're looking for a lower calorie and lower carb way to enjoy mac and cheese this recipe is for you. Spaghetti squash is cooked quickly in your electric pressure cooker and then a cheesy sauce is stirred in with the squash strands to make a comforting meal.

Ingredient: 1 spaghetti squash (small enough to fit in your Instant Pot when cut in half), 1/4 cup butter, 1/2 tsp. salt, 1/2 tsp. pepper, 1/2 tsp. garlic powder, 2 cups grated cheddar (I like sharp), 1/2 cup grated Parmesan cheese.

Preparation: Use a paring knife to cut your spaghetti squash in half crosswise (not lengthwise). Use a spoon to scoop out all the seeds and gunk. Pour a cup of water into the bottom of your Instant Pot. Place the trivet in the bottom of the pot. Place the squash halves on top of the trivet. They can face up or down. You may have to manoeuvre them around to fit. Secure the lid on the Instant Pot and make sure the valve is set to "sealing." Set the manual (high pressure) timer to 7 minutes. Once the timer beeps remove the pressure quickly by moving the valve to "venting." Remove the lid and use a towel or hot pad to remove the squash. Use a fork to shred the flesh of the squash into long spaghetti-like strands. Dump the water out of your Instant Pot and remove the trivet. Turn your Instant Pot to the sauté setting. Melt the butter and add in the salt, pepper and garlic powder. Once butter is melted add in the flesh of the spaghetti squash. Coat the squash with the butter and seasonings. Then turn off the Instant Pot.

Stir in the cheeses until melted and creamy. Add additional salt and pepper to taste.

Instant Pot Lentil Stew: a comforting bowl of stew that can be make vegan or can be made with smoked sausage. Lentils cook so quickly in the electric pressure cooker! The leftovers make a great lunch the next day too.

Ingredient: 1 Tbsp. olive oil, 1 yellow onion, diced, 1 cup green or brown lentils, 3 cups chicken broth or vegetable broth, 2 tsp. garlic powder, 1 tsp. dried parsley, 1/2 tsp. dried basil, 1/2 tsp. dried oregano, 1/2 tsp. salt, 1/4 tsp. ground red pepper, 1 (14.5 oz.) can petite diced tomatoes, 1 Tbsp. tomato paste, 1 large carrot, diced

Optional: 10 ounces beef smoked sausage, sliced into quarter inch pieces.

Preparation: Turn your Instant Pot to the sauté function. When the display says HOT add in the oil. Swirl the pot around. Add in the onion and sauté for about 4 minutes. Add in the lentils, broth, garlic powder, parsley, basil, oregano, salt, red pepper, tomatoes, tomato paste, carrot, and sausage. Cover the pot and secure the lid. Make sure valve is set to sealing. Set the manual/pressure cook button to 5 minutes. Let the pot sit for 5-10 minutes and then move the valve to venting. Open the pot. Stir the stew and salt and pepper to taste. Ladle into bowls and serve.

Instant Pot/Slow Cooker Mexican Stuffed Peppers: bell peppers are stuffed with brown rice, black beans and salsa and cooked perfectly in your electric pressure cooker or your crockpot. You can make them vegetarian or with meat, it's up to you. Top with a dollop of sour cream and enjoy this healthy weeknight dinner.

Ingredient: 1 1/2 cups water (Instant Pot version only), 4 large green peppers or 5 medium green peppers, 1/2 cup uncooked instant brown rice, 2 cups picante sauce (I used mild), 1/2 tsp. salt, 1 tsp. cumin, 1 tsp. garlic powder, 1 (14 oz.) can black beans, rinsed and drained

Optional: 1 cup cooked and chopped chicken or 1 cup cooked ground beef or turkey

Grated cheddar and sour cream, for topping.

Preparation: Remove and discard the tops, seeds, and membranes of the bell peppers. In a bowl stir together the rice, picante sauce, salt, cumin, garlic powder, beans, and meat, if desired. Scoop the mixture into the hollowed out peppers. If using the Instant Pot: Pour 1 1/2 cups water in the bottom of your pot. Place a trivet in the bottom of the Instant Pot. Place the peppers on top of the trivet. You may have to arrange them to fit. Cover the pot and secure the lid. Make sure valve is set to sealing. Set the manual/pressure cook button to 6 minutes on high pressure. When the time is up let the pot sit for about 5-10 minutes before moving the valve to venting. Remove the lid. If using the slow cooker: arrange the filled peppers in the bottom of your slow cooker. Cover and cook on low for 5 hours or on high for 3 hours.

Serve the peppers topped with a bit of grated cheddar cheese and a dollop of sour cream, if desired.

Instant Pot Wheat Berry Salad: Instant Pot Wheat Berry Salad—The perfect summer salad for all picnics, potlucks and barbecues. Wheat berries with a lime dressing, black beans, avocados, grape tomatoes, red peppers, jicama, red onion and cilantro. It's got the crunch, the chewiness and the bright flavours all in one salad.

Ingredient: FOR THE WHEAT BERRIES— 1 cup wheat, 4 cups water, 1 tsp. salt.

FOR THE SALAD— 1 large avocado, diced, 1 1/2 cups cubed jicama, 1 small red onion, finely diced, red bell pepper, finely diced, 1 (15-ounce can) black beans, drained and rinsed, 2 cups grape or cherry tomatoes sliced in half, 1/2 cup lime juice, 1/3 cup chopped fresh cilantro, 1/4 cup extra-virgin olive oil, 1 teaspoon ground cumin, 1 tsp. salt, 1 teaspoon freshly ground black pepper.

Preparation: Cook the wheat berries. Place wheat berries, water, and salt into Instant Pot. Cover the pot and secure the lid. Make sure valve is set to sealing. Set the manual/pressure cook button to 30 minutes on high pressure. When time is up perform a quick release by moving the valve to venting. Pour the wheat into a sieve and run cold water over it. Set aside.

Toss it together. Combine the avocados, jicama, onion, bell pepper, wheat berries (cooked previously), black beans, tomatoes, lime juice, cilantro, olive oil, cumin, salt and pepper in a medium bowl and adjust seasonings to taste. Chill at least 30 minutes and up to overnight before serving.

Instant Pot Tomato Basil Parmesan Orzo: Instant Pot Tomato Basil Parmesan Orzo—orzo pasta is tossed with fresh basil, garlic, halved cherry tomatoes and parmesan cheese for a perfect side dish or meatless meal.

Ingredient: 1 Tbsp. olive oil, 1 yellow onion, diced, 4 garlic cloves, minced, 3 1/2 cup chicken broth (or vegetable broth), 2 1/3 cup uncooked orzo pasta, 1/2 tsp salt, 1/2 tsp pepper, 1/3 cup chopped fresh basil, 1 cup grated parmesan cheese, 1 pint cherry tomatoes, washed and sliced in half.

Preparation: Turn your Instant Pot to the sauté function. When the display says HOT add in the olive oil and swirl it around. Add in the diced onion and sauté for about 3-5 minutes. Add in the garlic and sauté for 30 seconds. Add in the chicken broth and scrape any bits off the bottom of the pot. Add in the orzo, salt and pepper. Turn off the sauté function.

Cover the pot and secure the lid. Make sure valve is set to sealing. Set the manual/pressure cook button to 1 minute on high pressure. When the time is up let the pot sit there for 5 minutes and then perform a quick release.

Remove the lid and stir in the basil, cheese and tomatoes. Scoop onto plates and enjoy!

Instant Pot Spinach Artichoke Mac and Cheese: Instant Pot Spinach Artichoke Mac and Cheese—creamy, cheesy pasta with fresh spinach and chopped artichokes is a perfect way to indulge while sneaking in some greens.

Ingredient: 3 3/4 cups chicken broth (or water or vegetable broth), 16 ounces (1 pound) cavatappi, cellentani or macaroni pasta, uncooked, 1/2 tsp. salt, 1 or 2 (14 oz.) cans artichoke hearts, drained and chopped, 10 oz. bag of fresh spinach, 8 ounces Monterey jack cheese, grated

1/2 cup grated or shredded parmesan cheese, 1/2 tsp. pepper, Red pepper flakes, optional.

Preparation: Pour chicken broth into Instant Pot. Add in the uncooked pasta and salt.

Cover and secure lid. Make sure valve is set to sealing. Set the manual/pressure cook button to 3 minutes on high pressure. When time is up let the pot sit there for 5-10 minutes and then move the valve to venting. Remove the lid.

Turn Instant Pot to sauté mode and add in the artichokes and spinach. Stir the spinach in until it is wilted and cooks down. Add in the Monterey jack cheese and the parmesan cheese and pepper. Stir until cheese is melted. Sprinkle in a bit of red pepper flakes, if desired.

Scoop onto serving dishes and enjoy.

Instant Pot Creamy Polenta With Roasted Tomatoes: Instant Pot Creamy Polenta with Roasted Tomatoes—easiest to make polenta ever, thanks to your electric pressure cooker! Creamy polenta is served hot with balsamic drizzled roasted tomatoes, mushrooms and garlic and then topped with tart goat cheese. A perfect meatless meal that will leave you feeling satisfied.

Ingredient: 5 cups water, 1 cup polenta/corn grits (not the instant kind), 1 tsp. salt, 10 ounces white mushrooms, sliced, 10 ounces cherry or grape tomatoes, halved, 2 Tbsp. olive oil, 1 Tbsp. balsamic vinegar, 1 Tbsp. minced garlic, Salt and pepper, 6 Tbsp. goat cheese, for serving.

Preparation: Add water, polenta and salt to your Instant Pot. Whisk. Cover the pot and make sure valve is set to sealing. Set the porridge button to 20 minutes (if you don't have a porridge button you can use the manual/pressure cook button for 20 minutes on high pressure).

Turn your oven to 400° F. While the polenta is cooking slice your vegetables. Add mushrooms, tomatoes, oil, balsamic vinegar and garlic to a large bowl. Toss to coat vegetables in the oil. Spread out the contents of bowl onto a sheet pan. Lightly salt and pepper. Cook in the oven for 15-20 minutes. Once the Instant Pot timer beeps, let the pressure release naturally for 10 minutes and then move the valve to venting to remove any remaining pressure. Carefully open the lid. Whisk the polenta until creamy.

Scoop into bowls and top with roasted veggies and top with 1 tablespoon of goat cheese.

Instant Pot Spinach Mushroom Pesto Pasta: Instant Pot Spinach Mushroom Pesto Pasta—an easy, tasty and fast meatless meal of your favourite type of pasta enveloped in a basil pesto sauce with plenty of sautéed mushrooms and spinach. Add bites of chicken if you prefer.

Ingredient: 1 Tbsp. canola oil, 8 oz. (1/2 lb.) white button mushrooms, chopped, 1/2 tsp. kosher salt, 1/2 tsp. black pepper, 8 oz. uncooked orecchiette pasta (or other pasta of your choice), 1 3/4 cups water, 5 oz. fresh spinach, 1/2 cup pesto, 1/3 cup grated mozzarella cheese or parmesan cheese (optional).

Preparation: Turn your Instant Pot to the sauté function. While it heats up, chop up your mushrooms. When the display reads HOT add in your oil. Then add in your mushrooms, salt and pepper and sauté for about 5 minutes. Add in your pasta and water. Cover and secure the lid into place. Make sure valve is set to sealing. Set the manual/pressure cook button to 5 minutes (if cooking with another type of pasta read my note below). When the time is up move the valve to venting. Remove the lid. Stir in the spinach. And then stir in the pesto and cheese. If there is too much liquid you can use a corn-starch slurry to thicken the sauce by mixing 1 Tbsp. of corn-starch with 1 Tbsp. of water and then stirring the mixture into the pot.

Scoop the pasta into serving dishes and enjoy! Store leftovers in an airtight container in the refrigerator for up to a week.

COMFORT FOOD FAVOURITE.

Instant Pot Vegan Quinoa Burrito Bowls: This Mexican-inspired dish features protein-rich quinoa and black beans mixed with spicy salsa.

Ingredient: 1 teaspoon extra-virgin olive oil, 1/2 red onion, diced, 1 bell pepper, diced, 1/2 teaspoon salt, 1 teaspoon ground cumin, 1 cup quinoa, rinsed well, 1 cup prepared salsa, 1 cup water, 1 1/2 cups cooked black beans, or 1 (15 oz.) can, drained and rinsed, Optional toppings: Avocado, guacamole, fresh cilantro, green onions, salsa, lime wedges, shredded lettuce.

Preparation: Heat the oil in the bottom of the Instant Pot, using the "sauté" setting. Sauté the onions and peppers until start to soften, about 5 to 8 minutes, then add in cumin and salt and sauté another minute. Turn of the Instant Pot for a moment. Add in the quinoa, salsa, water, and beans, then seal the lid, making sure that the switch at the top is flipped from venting to sealing. Press the "rice" button, or manually cook at low pressure for 12 minutes. Let the pressure naturally release once the cooking is over, to make sure the quinoa completely absorbs the liquid. (This takes 10 to 15 minutes.) Remove the lid, being careful to avoid any steam releasing from the pot, and fluff the quinoa with a fork. Serve warm, with any toppings you love, such as avocado, diced onions, salsa, and shredded lettuce.

Leftovers can be stored in an airtight container in the fridge for up to a week. You can quickly reheat on the stove top, or serve cold!

Curried Butternut Squash Soup: Sautéed onions and creamy coconut milk make this lightly spiced (and quintessentially fall) soup extra flavourful.

Ingredient: 1 teaspoon extra-virgin olive oil, 1 large onion, chopped, 2 cloves garlic, minced

1 tablespoon curry powder, 1 (3 pound) butternut squash, peeled and cut into 1-inch cubes (or use frozen), 1 1/2 teaspoons fine sea salt, 3 cups water, 1/2 cup coconut milk (coconut cream is fine, too)

OPTIONAL TOPPINGS: Hulled pumpkin seeds, dried cranberries.

Preparation: Hit the "sauté" button on the Instant Pot. Add in the olive oil and onion, and sauté until tender, about 8 minutes. Add in the garlic and curry powder sauté just until fragrant, about one minute. Turn the Instant Pot off for a moment, then add the butternut squash, salt, and water into the pot. Secure the lid and move the steam release valve to "sealing." Select the Manual or Pressure Cook button (this will vary by machine, but they do the same thing) and let the soup cook at high pressure for 15 minutes.

When the soup is done, wait 10 minutes before releasing the pressure. When the screen reads LO:10, you can move the steam release valve to "venting" to release any remaining pressure. When the floating valve in the lid drops, it's safe to open the lid.

Use an immersion blender to puree the soup directly in the pot, or transfer the cooked soup to a blender or food processor to blend until smooth. If using a blender, be sure to lightly cover the vent in your blender lid with a dish towel, to help the pressure from the steam release without splattering. (The pressure from hot liquids can blow the lid off your blender otherwise, and cause burns.)

Return the blended soup to the pot and stir in the coconut milk. (You can use coconut cream, if you don't mind a slightly creamier soup.) Adjust any seasoning to taste at this point, I usually add a touch more salt, and serve warm. Top with hulled pumpkin seeds and dried cranberries, if desired. For a sweeter soup, try adding a touch of maple syrup to taste.

Leftovers can be stored in an airtight container for up to a week in the fridge.

The Best Instant Pot Mac and Cheese: This dish is perfect for one of those snowy Sunday evenings after a day on the slopes or an afternoon reading by the fire.

Ingredient: 1 pound macaroni, 4 cups water, 2 teaspoons prepared yellow mustard, 1 teaspoon salt, 12 ounce can evaporated milk, 8 ounces Tillamook medium cheddar cheese grated, ¾ cup parmesan cheese grated, 2 Tablespoons butter, ¼ teaspoon nutmeg, Salt and pepper to taste.

Preparation: Mix the macaroni, water, mustard, and salt in your Instant Pot. Close and lock the lid of the Instant Pot. Press "Manual" and adjust the timer to 4 minutes (or half the time on the macaroni cooking directions). Check that the cooking pressure is on "high" and that the release valve is set to "Sealing". When time is up, open the Instant Pot using "Quick Pressure Release". Stir the pasta to break it up. Add the evaporated milk, cheese, butter and nutmeg; stir until completely incorporated and then, cheese has melted and coated the pasta.

Season to taste with salt and pepper, then serve immediately.

Instant Pot Cheesy South-western Lentils and Brown Rice: Simmered with diced tomatoes and green chili, this stew is chock full of flavour. Add in some melted sharp cheddar and mozzarella and you'll be good to go.

Ingredient: 1/2 red onion finely chopped, 1/2 red bell pepper finely chopped, 4 garlic cloves minced, 3/4 cup Bob's Red Mill brown rice, 3/4 cup Bob's Red Mill brown lentils, 2 1/2 cups vegetable broth, 1 can petite diced tomatoes 15 oz., 1 can diced green chillies 4 oz., 1 Tbsp. taco seasoning, 2 tsp. dried oregano, 1 tsp. kosher salt, 1/2 tsp. Black pepper, 2 cups shredded cheese I prefer mozzarella and sharp cheddar, 1/4 cup chopped fresh cilantro for topping.

Preparation: Add all ingredients, except cheese and cilantro, to your Instant Pot. Set to manual and cook on high pressure for 15 minutes. Allow pressure to naturally release for 15 minutes then release remaining pressure. Remove cover and stir in half of the cheese. Sprinkle remaining cheese over the top and replace the cover. Allow to stand for 5 minutes.

Sprinkle with cilantro and serve. Enjoy!

Cauliflower Tikka Masala: With a mix of Indian spices and a flavourful, creamy base, this vegan veggie stew will transform weeknight dinner forever.

Ingredient: 1 tbsp. vegan butter (or oil), 1 medium onion, diced, 3 cloves of garlic, minced, 1 tbsp. freshly grated ginger, 2 tsp. dried fenugreek leaves, 2 tsp. gram masala, 1 tsp. turmeric, 1/2 tsp. ground chili, 1/4 tsp. ground cumin, 1/2 tsp. salt, 1 28-ounce can diced tomatoes with their juice (about 3 cups), 1 tbsp. (15ml) maple syrup, 1 small cauliflower head, cut into florets (about 4 cups florets), 1/2 cup (118ml) non-dairy yogurt (or cashew cream)

Optional toppings: fresh parsley, roasted cashews.

Preparation: Set the Instant Pot to sauté mode for 7 minutes. Add the oil. Once hot, add the onion, garlic, and ginger. Cook for 3-4 minutes, or until the onions start to caramelize and become soft. Add the dried fenugreek leaves, gram masala, turmeric, chili, cumin, and salt. Continue to cook for another 2 minutes, stirring regularly to make sure it doesn't burn. Add a couple of tablespoons of water and scrape the bottom to make sure nothing is sticking to it, this will prevent the Instant Pot from giving you a "burn" message.

Add the crushed tomatoes, maple syrup, and cauliflower florets. Secure the lid and close the vent to Sealing. Press the Pressure Cook button and adjust the time to 2 minutes. The Instant Pot will take about 10 minutes to come to pressure, then cook under pressure for 2 minutes. Once the program is finished and you have heard the beeps, wait 1 minute and release the pressure. Stir in the non-dairy yogurt and stir to combine.

Serve hot with rice, Nan, or tofu, and top with fresh parsley and roasted cashews.

Instant Pot Sesame Basil Noodles with Roasted Veggies: Infused with nutty sesame oil and spicy ginger, this Asian-inspired noodle dish is perfect for a quick and easy dinner on the go (and it's great for leftovers the next day.).

Ingredient: *ROASTED VEGGIES*— 1 bell pepper, diced, 1 (about 300g) sweet potato, peeled and diced, 1 head broccoli, cut into florets, 1 tbsp. (15ml) olive oil, 1 tbsp. (15ml) soy sauce, 1/4 tsp. ground ginger, 1/4 tsp. ground chili powder.

NOODLES— 8 ounces (227g) linguine pasta, broken in half, 2 cups and 2 tbsp. (500ml) water, 3 tbsp. (45ml) soy sauce, 1 and 1/2 tbsp. sesame oil, 1 tbsp. (15ml) chili oil, 1 tbsp. (15ml) maple syrup, 1 tbsp. (15ml) white rice vinegar, 1 clove of garlic, minced, 1/8 tsp. five-spice powder (optional), 1/4 cup (6g) fresh basil, chopped.

For topping: sesame seeds, basil.

Preparation: Preheat oven to 400°F (200°C) and line a baking sheet with parchment paper.

Add the diced bell pepper, sweet potato, and broccoli to a large mixing bowl. Pour in the olive oil, and soy sauce and add the ground ginger and chili powder. Mix using your hands to coat the vegetables with the oil and spices. Transfer the veggies to the prepared baking sheet and spread into an even layer. Bake for 20-22 minutes, or until veggies are slightly browned. While the veggies are roasting, prepare the noodles.

NOODLES— add the noodles broken in half to the Instant Pot liner. Then add the water, soy sauce, sesame oil, chili oil, maple syrup, rice vinegar, minced garlic, five-spice powder if using, and fresh basil leaves. Close the lid and pressure cook on manual for 8 minutes. Let the pressure release naturally for 3 minutes before doing a quick release of the steam.

Transfer the roasted veggies to the Instant Pot liner and mix until combined. Serve immediately topped with fresh basil and sesame seeds.

Lentil Sloppy Joes: For a healthier, veggie-based version of the traditional ground beef classic, try this innovative vegan recipe with a secret ingredient (liquid smoke!).

Ingredient: 1 tablespoon oil (Instant Pot or stovetop only, optional, see note below), 1 small, yellow onion diced, 3 garlic cloves minced, 2 teaspoons oregano, 1 teaspoon paprika, 1 tablespoon chili powder, 1 teaspoon salt, 1/2 teaspoon ground black pepper, 1 cup dry brown lentils, 1 1/2 cups vegetable broth or water, 1 28-oz can no salt added crushed tomatoes, 2 tablespoons tomato paste, 1 tablespoon yellow mustard, 3 tablespoons vegan Worcestershire sauce, 1/2 teaspoon liquid smoke (optional, see note below), 1-2 tablespoons pure maple syrup (optional).

Preparation: Set your Instant Pot to the Sauté function. Add oil. Once the oil is hot, add the onions and sauté for 2 minutes. Add the garlic. Sauté for another 2 minutes. Add the oregano, paprika, chili powder, salt, and pepper. Mix until spices have coated the onions and garlic. Cancel the sauté function.

Add the brown lentils, the broth or water, crushed tomatoes, tomato paste, yellow mustard, and vegan Worcestershire sauce. Stir until everything has combined.

Lock the lid in place and make sure the steam release handle is closed. Set to manual high pressure for 12 minutes. Instant Pot will take roughly 10 minutes to build pressure, timer will start counting down after it has reached pressure. After the time has ended, let the pressure release naturally, this will take roughly 20 minutes. Once the pressure has been released naturally (you will know pressure has been released when the float valve has dropped back down), slowly unlock and remove the lid. Stir so everything combines.

If using, add the liquid smoke, stir and taste. If you find it too acidic, add maple syrup, starting with 1 tablespoon, to balance it out. Stir to combine and taste again. Add another tablespoon of maple syrup, if needed. Serve on rolls of your choice with toppings and sides of your choice (see above for suggestions).

Instant Pot Artichokes with Lemon Chive Butter: The Instant Pot isn't just for soups and stews. It's also an easy way to cook tough vegetables like steamed artichokes, which pair perfectly with a lemon and herb dipping sauce.

Ingredient: 3 large globe artichokes, 1/2 lemon, 2 tablespoons extra-virgin olive oil, 4 tablespoons butter, melted, 2 tablespoons lemon juice, 2 tablespoons minced fresh chives, 1/8 teaspoon kosher salt.

Preparation: Use a serrated edge knife to cut an inch off the top of the artichokes and cut off the stems. Rub the half lemon over the artichokes where they've been cut to prevent browning. Use scissors to trim any sharp tips from the tips of the leaves. Pour 1 1/2 cups water into the Instant Pot with the metal insert in place. Set the artichokes in the pot, stem-side-up. Cover and set to Manual/High for 13 minutes with the vent closed.

Release the steam with care and open the pot. Test to see if the artichokes are done by tasting a leaf or two and inserting the tip of a knife in the stem.

It should slide in with relative ease. If they're not quite done, cook another 1 to 2 minutes. Whisk together the olive oil, melted butter, lemon juice, chives, and salt. Serve with the artichokes.

Instant Pot Broccoli Cheddar Quiche: Eggs are a mainstay ingredient for many vegetarians; they're filled with protein and a delicious foil to healthy veggies and tangy cheeses, like in this easy quiche recipe.

Ingredient: 6 large eggs, ½ cup whole milk, ½ teaspoon kosher salt, ¼ teaspoon freshly ground black pepper, 1 small head broccoli about 8 ounces, finely chopped, 3 green onions white and light green parts, sliced, 1 cup shredded Cheddar cheese 4 ounces.

Preparation: Butter a 1½-quart soufflé dish or a 7-cup round heatproof glass container. Fold a 20-inch-long sheet of aluminium foil in half lengthwise twice to create a 3-inch-wide strip. Centre it underneath the soufflé dish to act as a sling for lifting the dish into and out of the Instant Pot. Pour 1 1/2cups water into the pot and add the trivet. In a bowl, whisk together the eggs, milk, salt, and pepper. Stir in the broccoli, green onions, and cheese.

Pour the egg mixture into the prepared dish. Then, holding the ends of the foil sling, lift the dish and lower it into the Instant Pot. Fold over the ends of the sling so they fit inside the pot. Secure the lid and set the Pressure Release to Sealing. Select Manual setting and set the cooking time for 25 minutes at high pressure. Let the pressure release naturally for at least 10 minutes, then move the Pressure Release to Venting to release any remaining steam. Open the pot and, wearing heat-resistant mitts, grasp the ends of the foil sling and lift the quiche out of the Instant Pot. Let the quiche cool for at least 5 minutes, giving it time to reabsorb any liquid and set up.

Slice and serve warm or at room temperature.

Coconut Jasmine Rice: Rice is another ingredient that can be totally transformed using the Instant Pot. This vegan and gluten-free recipe is a great side dish for a veggie stir-fry or other hearty main course.

Ingredient: 2 cups Jasmine rice, 1 can reduced-fat coconut milk, (Lite coconut milk) 13.5 ounces, 1 cup water, 1 Tablespoon lime juice, 1 cup frozen peas, defrosted.

Preparation: Rinse the rice in a mesh strainer. Add the rice to the Instant Pot along with the coconut milk and water. Stir to combine. Close the lid and push the Rice function button. If you have a display, it will show as 12 minutes at low pressure. Note that the cooking time may adjust once the Instant Pot has come up to pressure.

After the rice is done cooking, allow the pressure to release naturally. After the pressure has released, remove the lid and add in the lime juice and peas. Use a rice paddle to gently fold all the ingredients together until well combined.

Let rest for a few minutes, then serve.

Cilantro Lime Quinoa: Ready in just 15 minutes, this bright side dish features lime juice and zest for added flavour.

Ingredient: 1 cup quinoa, (any colour) rinsed and drained, 1 1/4 cups vegetable broth, (for Instant Pot method) or 2 cups for stove top method, 2 Tablespoons lime juice, zest of one lime, 1/2 cup chopped cilantro, salt, to taste.

Preparation: Add the quinoa and 1 1/4 cup vegetable broth to the Instant Pot. Close the lid and select the manual button. Set the timer for 5 minutes.

When the 5 minutes is up, allow the pressure to release naturally.

Once the pressure has been released, remove the lid and stir in the lime juice, lime zest, and cilantro. Taste and add salt, as desired.

VEGAN LUNCH RECIPES BY INSTANT POT.

Smoky Sweet Pecan Brussels sprouts: a little bit sweet, a little bit smoky, with a nutty crunch. And they only take about 15 minutes to make!

Ingredient: 2 cups small baby Brussels sprouts - 176 g, as close to the same size as possible, ¼, cup water - 60 ml, 1/2 teaspoon liquid smoke

Sauté Ingredients— 1/4 cup chopped pecans - 28 g, 2 tablespoons maple syrup - 30 ml, salt - to taste.

Preparation: For the pressure cooker, add the Brussels sprouts, water and liquid smoke to your Instant Pot and mix well. Put the lid on and close the pressure valve. Cook on high pressure for 2 minutes. (Note: If you have very large Brussels sprouts, you may need to double the cooking time.) Once the cooking time is up, carefully move the pressure release valve to release the pressure manually.

For the sauté, switch to the sauté function and add in the pecans and maple syrup and reduce the liquid as you finish cooking the sprouts. Remove from the heat once tender and add salt to taste.

Instant Pot Stuffed Squash with Wild Rice: The key ingredient that makes this stuffed acorn squash healthy and filling is chickpeas. Canned chickpeas are one of my pantry staples. They are inexpensive, rich in fibre and protein, and incredibly versatile.

Ingredient: 1/2 cup uncooked wild rice — you can also use a brown and wild rice blend like this one, 1 teaspoon kosher salt — divided, 3 small — 1 pound each acorn squashes, halved lengthwise, stems trimmed, and seeded, 1 tablespoon olive oil, 1 medium shallot — finely chopped, or 1/2 small yellow onion, finely chopped, 3 large cloves garlic — minced (about 1 tablespoon), 8 ounces baby Bella — cremini mushrooms, finely chopped, 1/2 teaspoon black pepper, 1 can reduced-sodium chickpeas — (15 ounces) rinsed and drained, 1/3 cup reduced-sugar dried cranberries, 1/4 cup toasted pepitas — or chopped pecans, 1 tablespoon fresh thyme leaves — chopped.

Preparation: Bring 1 1/2 cups water to a boil in a small saucepan. Add the rice and 1/2 teaspoon kosher salt. Reduce heat to low, cover, and let simmer until the rice is tender, about 55 minutes. Drain off any excess liquid. Set aside.

Pour 1/2 cup water into the bottom of an Instant Pot or electric pressure cooker. Place the steamer basket in the pot, then add the squash, cut sides up (they will overlap). Be sure not to exceed the max fill line. If your squash are larger and you exceed the line, cook the squash in two batches. Seal the lid, set pressure valve to sealing, and cook on HIGH (manual) for 4 minutes. Allow the pressure to release naturally for 5 minutes, then immediately vent to release any remaining pressure. Drain and arrange on a large serving plate or baking sheet.

Meanwhile, heat the olive oil in a large skillet over medium low. Add the shallot and cook until softened, about 4 minutes. Add the garlic and cook 30 seconds until fragrant, then add the mushrooms, black pepper, and remaining 1/2 teaspoon kosher salt. Increase heat to medium and cook until the mushrooms are softened and browned, about 5 to 7 additional minutes. Add the chickpeas, cranberries, pepitas, thyme, and cooked rice and stir to heat through, about 2 additional minutes. Taste and adjust seasonings as desired.

Spoon the hot filling into the squash halves. Serve immediately or keep warm in a 350 degree F oven.

Seasoned Black Beans: This Instant Pot Black Beans recipe makes a simple, tasty, healthy & budget friendly lunch. As well as being great on their own, they work equally as well as a base for other meals, so are perfect for meal prep!

Ingredient: 450g / 2½ cups dried black beans , no need to soak before using, 1 medium onion , chopped finely, 4 cloves garlic , chopped finely, 1 teaspoon chili flakes , or 1 fresh chili, (you can omit the chili if you prefer), 1 tablespoon ground cumin, 1 teaspoon ground coriander, 1 large bay leaf, 1 teaspoon dried mint , optional but recommended if you have it, 720 mls / 3 cups flavourful broth/stock, 1 lime, juice only, up to 1 teaspoon salt , plus more to taste if required.

Preparation: Add all ingredients except the lime to the Instant Pot and stir. Put the lid on the Instant Pot and seal the vent. Cook on high pressure MANUAL or PRESSURE COOK in newer models, for 25 minutes for tender, soft beans, (or 30 minutes of you prefer really soft slightly mushy beans) and leave the pressure to release naturally before opening the lid.

Please note that the beans continue to cook during the natural pressure release so if you skip this step and vent manually your beans will turn out much firmer. Add salt to taste then squeeze the juice of the lime into the beans and give them a quick stir before serving.

Instant Pot Maple Bourbon Sweet Potato Chili: A sweet and spicy soup with a kick, this Maple Bourbon Sweet Potato Instant Pot Chili is the perfect autumnal vegan and gluten-free family meal.

Ingredient: 1 tbsp. cooking oil, 1 small yellow onion, thinly sliced, 2-3 cloves garlic minced, 4 cups sweet potatoes, peeled and cubed into 1/2 pieces, 2 cups vegetable broth, 1 1/2 tbsp. chili powder, 2 tsp. cumin, 1/2 tsp. paprika, 1/4 tsp. cayenne pepper, 2 (15) ounce cans kidney beans, drained and rinsed, 1 (15) ounce can diced tomatoes, 1/4 cup bourbon, 2 tbsp. maple syrup, salt and pepper, to taste, a few fresh springs of cilantro, 2 green onions, diced, 3 small corn tortillas, toasted and sliced (optional).

Preparation: Turn your Instant Pot to sauté, add oil, and let it heat up for 30 seconds. Once the oil is hot, add onions and sauté for about 5 minutes, stirring occasionally, until onions are translucent and fragrant. Add garlic and sauté for another 30 seconds. Add cubed sweet potatoes, chili powder, cumin, paprika, and cayenne pepper, stirring until vegetables are well coated. Add vegetable broth, beans, tomatoes, maple syrup, and bourbon. Secure the lid on the Instant Pot and set the mode to "soup". Set a timer for 15 minutes. Once the timer goes off, lid should release itself. If it doesn't, turn the air valve to "venting" until the pressure has been released. Remove lid and check to make sure the sweet potatoes are tender. If using tortillas, lightly oil a cast iron skillet and pan-fry the tortillas on each side for 2-3 minutes until crispy. Remove from heat and let cool before cutting into thin strips.

Serve with cilantro, green onions, and toasted tortillas.

Instant Pot Walnut Lentil Tacos: I love these most wrapped in a flour tortilla with lots of shredded lettuce and salsa, but they also taste great over a loaded salad with crunchy tortilla chips. Either way, it's a healthy, protein-packed weeknight meal that you are sure to love.

Ingredient: 1 white onion, diced, 1 tablespoon olive oil, 1 garlic clove, minced, 1 tablespoon chili powder, 1/2 teaspoon garlic powder, 1/4 teaspoon onion powder, 1/4 teaspoon red pepper flakes, 1/4 teaspoon oregano, 1/2 teaspoon paprika, 1 1/2 teaspoon ground cumin, 1/2 teaspoon kosher salt, 1/4 teaspoon freshly ground pepper, 2 1/4 cups vegetable broth, 1 15 ounce can fire-roasted diced tomatoes, 3/4 cup chopped walnuts, 1 cup dried brown lentils, Taco toppings of choice: shredded lettuce, tomato, jalapenos, Flour or corn tortillas.

Preparation: Turn the Instant Pot on and press the Sauté button. Add the olive oil, onion and garlic clove and sauté until onion is tender and cooked through, stirring often, about 3-4 minutes. Add the spices and stir together.

Hit cancel and add the vegetable broth, tomatoes, walnuts and lentils and stir to combine. Place the top on and cook on high manual pressure for 15 minutes. Let pressure come down naturally for 4 minutes, then quick release. Remove the lid and stir lentils, seasoning to taste if needed.

Serve lentils on tortillas of choice with toppings. The lentil mixture will thicken as it cools.

Instant Pot Quinoa Enchiladas: What do we call this? It's got all the flavours of enchiladas, but it's definitely not enchiladas. No rolling, no filling, no baking. Just throwing all of the ingredients in the pressure cooker and in 25 minutes, lunch is served.

Ingredient: 3 tablespoons oil (use canola), 3 tablespoons all-purpose flour (see notes for GF version), 1 tablespoon chili powder, 1 1/2 teaspoons cumin, 1/2 teaspoon oregano, 1/2 teaspoon garlic powder, 1/4 teaspoon salt, 1/8 teaspoon cinnamon, 1/4 teaspoon cayenne pepper, 1 (15 ounce) can crushed tomatoes, 1 cup water (or vegetable broth).

Enchilada Ingredients: 2 bell peppers, chopped, 1 medium onion, chopped, 1 cup enchilada sauce, 1 medium zucchini, chopped, 1 cup uncooked quinoa, 3/4 cup water, 1 (15 ounce) can black beans, drained and rinsed, 1 (15 ounce) can corn, drained and rinsed, 1 (4 ounce) can diced jalapeños, 1/4 cup fresh cilantro, 4 corn tortillas, cut into strips, 1 cup shredded cheddar cheese

Preparation: Make the enchilada sauce: heat the oil in a medium saucepan over medium heat. Stir in the flour and cook until golden brown, about 3-4 minutes stirring often. Add in the rest of the spices: chili powder, cumin, garlic powder, oregano, salt, cinnamon, and cayenne and stir another minute until toasted. Whisk in the crushed tomatoes and water and stir until thickened, about 5-7 minutes. Remove 1 cup of the sauce and set the rest aside for drizzling over finished dish or for later. (This sauce freezes beautifully!) Turn the Instant Pot on and hit the sauté button. Add the bell peppers, onion, zucchini and a drizzle of olive oil and pinch of salt. Cook, stirring often, until vegetables are soft. Add in the uncooked quinoa and cook another minute or two until just toasted. Press the cancel button on the Instant Pot and add in the water and 1 cup of the enchilada sauce. Cover and cook at high pressure for 1 minute, then let the pressure come down naturally.

Remove the lid and immediately once pressure has subsided (about 15 minutes) then stir in the black beans, corn, jalapeno, cheese, and cilantro and corn tortillas. Serve hot, with extra enchilada sauce if desired

Instant Pot Apple Spice Steel Cut Oats: Substitute almond milk for cow's milk and you've got one heck of a vegan lunch.

Ingredient: 1 cup steel cut oats, 1/2 cup unsweetened plain applesauce, 1 teaspoon ground cinnamon, 1/2 teaspoon ground nutmeg, 1/4 teaspoon salt, 3 cups water, 1 small apple, chopped, 1/2 cup raisins (optional), chopped nuts, or fresh diced or sliced apples for garnish (optional), milk (enough to reach desired consistency), sweetener, to taste (optional).

Preparation: Add steel cut oats, applesauce, ground cinnamon, ground nutmeg, salt, and water to your Instant Pot. Stir to combine all the ingredients. Lock the lid in place and make sure the steam release handle is closed. Set to manual high pressure for 10 minutes. Instant Pot will take roughly 10 minutes to build pressure, timer will start counting down after it has reached pressure. After the time has ended, let the Instant Pot naturally release the pressure. This will take roughly 20 minutes.

Once the pressure has been released naturally (you will know pressure has been released when the float valve has dropped back down), slowly unlock and remove the lid. Stir the oats so everything recombines. Add the apples and, if using, raisins, and stir. Let sit for a minute or two so apples (and raisins) can warm up. Add desired amount of milk and stir. Add sweetener, to taste. Sprinkle nuts and/or fresh fruit on top for garnish.

Instant Pot Vegan Lentil Chili: Thick, hearty and packed with plant-based protein. You're going to love this Instant Pot vegan lentil chili.

Ingredient: 1 tablespoon olive oil, 1 onion, chopped, 4 cloves minced garlic, 2 carrots, chopped, 1–2 jalapeños, chopped, 1 1/2 tablespoons chili powder, 1 tablespoon cumin, 1/2 teaspoon ground coriander, 1 teaspoon dried oregano, 1/2–3/4 teaspoon salt, 1 (15 ounce) can crushed tomatoes, 1 (28 ounce) can fire roasted diced tomatoes, 2 cups brown or green lentils (I used French green lentils for this, I find they hold their shape best), 4 cups vegetable broth, 1 teaspoon fresh lime juice, 1/2 cup chopped fresh cilantro

Preparation: Press the sauté button on the Instant Pot. Heat the olive oil in the pot, then add the onion, garlic, carrots and jalapeños and sauté until soft, about 3-4 minutes.

Add the spices and remaining ingredients except for lime juice and cilantro, then cover. Cook on high pressure for 15 minutes, then quick-release.

Stir in lime juice and cilantro, and serve.

Instant Pot Vegan Butter Chicken: The garnish of fresh minced ginger and chili and some dried fenugreek takes this dish to an amazing flavour level. Make it!

Ingredient: 3 large ripe tomatoes or 1 15 oz. can diced tomatoes, 4 cloves of garlic, 1/2 inch (0.5 inch) cube of ginger, 1 hot or mild green chili , I use Serrano, 3/4 cup (250 ml) water , use 1, cup if the tomatoes aren't very juicy, ½ to 1 tsp. (1/2 to 1 tsp.) garam masala, ½ tsp. (0.5 tsp.) paprika or Kashmiri chili powder, ¼ to ½ tsp. (1/4 to 1/2 tsp.) cayenne, 3/4 tsp. (0.75 tsp.) salt, 1 cup (55 g) soy curls (dry, not rehydrated), 1 cup (5.78 oz.) cooked chickpeas, Cashew cream made with ¼ cup soaked cashews blended with ½ cup water, 1/2 tsp. (0.5 tsp.) or more garam masala, 1/2 tsp. (0.5 tsp.) or more sugar or sweetener, 1 tsp. kasoori methi - dried fenugreek leaves or add a 1/4 tsp. ground mustard, 1/2 (0.5) moderately hot green chili finely chopped, or use 2 tbsp. finely chopped green bell pepper, 1/2 tsp. (0.5 tsp.) minced or finely chopped ginger, 1/4 cup (4 g) cilantro for garnish.

Preparation: Blend the tomatoes, garlic, ginger, chili with water until smooth.

Add pureed tomato mixture to the Instant pot or pressure cooker. Add soy curls, chickpeas, spices and salt. Close the lid and cook on Manual for 8 to 10 minutes. Quick release after 10 minutes. Start the IP on sauté (medium heat for stove top pressure cooker). Add the cashew cream, garam masala, sweetener and fenugreek leaves and mix in. Bring to a boil, taste and adjust salt, heat, sweet. Add more cayenne and salt if needed. Fold in the chopped green chili, ginger and cilantro and press cancel (take off heat).

At this point you can add some vegan butter or oil for additional buttery flavour. Serve hot over rice or with flatbread or Naan.

Fluffy Mashed Potatoes with Vegan Gravy: Mashed Potatoes don't need an introduction. They are used is many cuisines in many different ways. These are basic mashed potatoes that you can amp up to preference.

Ingredient: 5 to 6 potatoes cubed into large pieces Yukon gold or baking potatoes, peeled if desired, 5 cloves of garlic, 1/2 tsp. (0.5 tsp.) salt, 1 tbsp. extra virgin olive oil or vegan butter, a good dash of black pepper, dash of parsley or thyme, pinch of nutmeg, 1 cup (226 ml) full fat coconut milk, fresh chives for garnish.

preparation: Pressure cook the cubed potatoes, garlic cloves, 1/4 tsp. salt with 1.5 cups water at high pressure for 4 minutes in Instant pot (manual 4 mins) or 2 minutes in stove top pressure cooker. Release the pressure after 5 minutes. (You can also boil them in a saucepan. Put the potatoes into a large pot, adding enough water to cover them. Bring to a boil and simmer for 10-15 mins, until they're fork-tender. Transfer to a colander to drain.)

Drain really well. Transfer to a bowl, let sit for a few minutes to dry out. Mash lightly and let sit for a minute for the steam to escape. Make sure to mash the cooked garlic. Mix in salt, the rest of the ingredients and half cup coconut milk. Mix and whip lightly, just enough to add air and still have some texture. Let sit for a minute for the milks to incorporate and absorb.

Taste and adjust. Add 1/4 tsp. or more salt as needed. Add more coconut milk for creamier consistency to preference if needed and mix in. Add 1-2 tbsp. nutritional yeast for cheesy potatoes. Garnish with chives.

Instant Pot Artichokes: Easy, Fast, Fool proof Artichokes Recipe in 20 mins! Super food nutrient powerhouse with delicious delicate flavours.

Ingredient: 2 artichokes (1/2lb, 250g each, 11" circumference), 4 cloves (13g) garlic, minced, 2 tablespoons (30g) unsalted butter, Kosher Salt to taste (about 2 pinches) Optional: lemon juice from 1 lemon.

Preparation: Wash Artichokes: Submerge artichokes in cold water for 5 minutes.

Optional - Prep Artichokes: Cut stem off and trim about 1 inch off the tip of the artichokes.

Place Artichokes in Pressure Cooker— Place 1 cup of cold water and a steamer rack in the Instant Pot pressure cooker. Place 2 whole artichokes on the steamer rack, and close the lid.

Optional: If you like, squeeze some lemon juice on the artichokes to slow the rate of oxidation.

Pressure Cook Artichokes: Pressure cook

a) Trimmed Artichokes: High Pressure for 8 minutes (using the Manual Button/Pressure Cook) + Quick Release OR

b) Uncut Whole Artichokes: High Pressure for 9 minutes (using the Manual Button/Pressure Cook) + Quick Release

c) For Large Artichokes: Increase the pressure cooking time accordingly.

Open the lid carefully.

Prepare Garlic Butter: While the artichokes are cooking in the pressure cooker, heat a sauce pan over medium low heat. Melt 2 tbsp. (30g) unsalted butter and add in the minced garlic. Sauté garlic until golden brown. Do not let the garlic burn. Set aside to cool it down slightly. Season with kosher salt and adjust to taste (about 2 pinches).

Serve: Serve artichokes with Garlic Butter Sauce.

Note: use olive oil in place of unsalted butter for dipping sauce.

CILANTRO LIME BROWN RICE: The flavour of this rice is so spot on, and using brown rice made it feel way less guilty going back for seconds.

Ingredient: 1 cup Uncooked Long-grain Brown Rice, 1 teaspoon Butter, 2 cloves Garlic, Minced, 5 teaspoons Fresh Lime Juice, Divided, 1 can (15 Oz. Size) Vegetable Broth, 1 cup Water, 4 Tablespoons Fresh Cilantro, Chopped.

Preparation: In a saucepan add the rice, butter, garlic, 2 teaspoons of lime juice, broth and water; stir to combine. Bring the rice mixture to a boil, then reduce heat to low, cover and cook for 40 minutes, until rice is tender. While rice is cooking, whisk the remaining 3 teaspoons (or 1 tablespoon) lime juice and cilantro together in a small bowl. When rice is ready, remove it from the heat and pour the lime/cilantro mixture over the rice, mixing it in as you fluff the rice. Serve immediately.

VEGAN BREAKFAST RECIPES BY INSTANT POT.

Start your day with one of these Easy Instant Pot vegan breakfast recipes and you'll be surprised at good you feel. When you start off your day right it's so much easier to eat right all day long.

Stuffed sweet potatoes: These Instant Pot Breakfast Stuffed Sweet Potatoes are an easy, healthy, vegan way to start your day! They're quickly cooked in a pressure cooker, then stuffed with almond butter, maple syrup, and blueberries!

Ingredient: 1 cup water, 1 sweet potato, 1 tablespoon pure maple syrup, 1 tablespoon almond butter, 1 tablespoon chopped pecans, 2 tablespoons blueberries, 1 teaspoon chia seeds.

Preparation: Place the steamer rack in your instant pot and add one cup of water. Place the sweet potato on the rack and seal the lid, making sure the release valve is in the proper position. Set the Instant Pot to manual high pressure for 15 minutes. It will take a few minutes to come up to pressure.

Once the time is up, allow the pressure to release naturally for ten minutes. Turn the release valve to release any leftover pressure. Once the float valve has dropped, open the lid and remove the sweet potato. When it is cool enough to handle, cut the sweet potato and mash the flesh with a fork. Drizzle with maple syrup and almond butter, then sprinkle with pecans, blueberries, and chia seeds.

Uttapams savoury Indian pancakes: It's a savoury Indian pancake that's easy to make and actually is inexpensive too. My whole foods recipe uses healthy grains and lentils that ferment into a flavourful batter overnight.

Ingredient: 1 cup urad dal, 1 cup brown rice, 1 cup millet, 1 cup quinoa, washed well to remove the seed coating, 5 cups water.

Preparation: Mix the urad dal, rice, millet, quinoa and water in a large bowl. Cover and let soak to soften for 8 hours. After the soak, puree the mixture (including the soaking water) in your blender in batches and add to your Instant Pot liner. Place the liner in your Instant Pot, cover and press the yogurt setting. Leave it at the default 8 hours for it to ferment.

Note: You can store the fermented mixture in your fridge for up to 1 week or you can cook up all the pancakes at once and freeze them to heat for later.

Heat a non-stick skillet over medium heat. Once hot, add ½ cup (120 ml) of the batter per pancake and shape into a circle. Cook until bubbles begin to form. Sprinkle the topping you choose over the top of the pancake and press in a little with your spatula. Flip the pancake and cook until both sides are browned. Place on a plate and cook the next one. You could also have more than one skillet going at a time.

INSTANT POT BREAKFAST POTATOES: Instant Pot breakfast potatoes are prepared ahead of time for a quick breakfast, brunch or even dinner. Season this savoury side in the IP then brown and crisp them on a skillet. They're easy to make and full of flavour!

Ingredient: 6 yukon gold or red potatoes, or 4 russets (roughly 2lbs), diced into 1/2-inch cubes, 2-3 Tablespoons refined coconut oil, or neutral oil of choice, 3/4 cup of water or vegetable broth, 1 Tablespoon nutritional yeast, 2 teaspoons garlic powder, 1 teaspoons onion powder, 1/4 teaspoon paprika, Himalayan pink salt to taste (I use about 3/4 teaspoon), Pepper to taste, neutral oil for sautéing, I use refined coconut oil, 1 small onion, 1 green bell pepper.

Preparation: In a small bowl combine the seasonings and set aside. Dice the potatoes into evenly sized cubes. Dry the cubed potatoes with a kitchen/paper towels to remove excess moisture.

Add the potatoes and oil to the IP and press the sauté feature. Sauté the potatoes just until they begin to change texture (about 5 minutes). The potatoes may stick so be sure to frequently stir them. Don't worry, any sticking will come up after pressure cooking and add extra flavour to the potatoes. Halfway through cooking mix-in the seasonings. Once the potatoes have started to change texture, press the cancel button on the IP. You don't want to over sauté them since they will be pressure cooked as well.

Pour in the water or broth, but don't mix. Secure the lid and make sure the steam vent is sealed. Set the IP to low pressure for 1 minute. Once done, carefully, quick release the steam vent. The potatoes may be undercooked, but they will fully cook when reheated in the skillet. Gently mix the potatoes to prevent mashing while scraping up any browning on the bottom of the pot. Let cool, then refrigerate for the next morning, or at least 2 hours.

Instant Pot Vegan Quinoa Breakfast Recipe: instant Pot Vegan Quinoa Breakfast Recipe is super yum & easy to put together. Vegan Quinoa Porridge is a quick make ahead recipe for breakfast or brunch.

Ingredient: 1 Cup Quinoa, 3 Cups Almond Milk, unsweetened, Toppings & Garnishes, 1/4 cup Maple Syrup, original, 1 Tbsp. Walnuts chopped, plain, 1/2 Tbsp. Pistachio chopped, plain, 1 Tbsp. Resins, and 2 Tbsp. Almonds chopped, plain, 1/2 Cup Fresh Berries of Choice.

Preparation: Place the inner pot inside the Instant Pot. Plug it in. Wash the quinoa under running cold water till water runs clear. Set aside. Place the washed quinoa and 3 cups of Almond Milk inside the Inner Pot. If you want slightly more liquid consistency, then add 5 cups of almond milk. You can also add more milk later once it is cooked to adjust the consistency to your liking. Place the Lid and lock it to SEALING. Select the Pressure Cook/Manual Mode and set it on HIGH for 2 MINUTES.

Once the timer goes off, follow NPR. Once the safety valve drops down, open the lid carefully. You will get the porridge of THICK CONSISTENCY. I liked this consistency. If you like little more runny porridge, then add more almond milk to it. Just warm the almond milk and add and stir. Use as required. Top your Quinoa Porridge with Maple Syrup, Fresh Berries and Dry Nuts. Enjoy a hearty Breakfast. It is a perfect example of Dessert for Breakfast too.

Pumpkin Coffeecake Steel-cut Oatmeal: This recipe for Instant Pot Vegan Pumpkin Coffeecake Steel-cut Oatmeal makes a ton. It's a departure from my usual recipes for two servings. You actually get 6 to 8 servings – enough to make once and grab breakfast from the fridge or freezer all week long.

Ingredient: 4 1/2 cups water, 1 1/2 cups steel-cut oats, 1 1/2 cups pumpkin puree or 1 15 oz. can, 2 teaspoons cinnamon, 1 teaspoon allspice, 1 teaspoon vanilla, 1/2 cup coconut sugar or brown sugar or sweetener of choice, to taste, 1/4 cup pecans or walnuts chopped, 1 tablespoon cinnamon.

Preparation: Add all the instant pot ingredients to your stainless steel insert and put it into the base. Secure the lid and make sure the valve is closed. Set on manual and cook for 3 minutes. While the oats are cooking, mix all the topping ingredients together and store in an airtight container.

Once the oats are cooked, allow the pressure to come down naturally.

Once the silver pressure indicator goes down you can open the lid.

Serve sprinkled with topping and/or your favourite non-dairy milk!

Instant Pot Steel Cut Oats Cooked with Earl Grey Tea: Earl Grey tea is the perfect cooking liquid for your morning oats. It adds the unique punch of flavour in my Instant Pot Earl Grey Steel Cut Oats. I suggest adding some rosewater, vanilla, or a little lavender extract to customize your steel cut oats even more!

Ingredient: 1 ½ cups brewed Earl Grey Tea, you can use black, decaf or rooibos, ½ cup steel- cut oats, ½ teaspoon rosewater, vanilla, or a few drops of lavender extract, sweetener of your choice, to taste.

Preparation: Add the brewed tea and oats to your Instant Pot. Put your lid on and make sure the vent is closed. Select the manual/pressure cooker setting and set to cook for 3 minutes.

Allow the pressure to release naturally. Open and mix in your choice of sweetener and extra flavouring. Serve topped with non-dairy milk.

Sprouted Lentils Bowl: Sprouted Lentils Breakfast Bowl — A perfect make-ahead, meatless breakfast with protein-rich sprouted brown lentils, lightly spiced with freshly grated ginger, turmeric, mild red Kashmiri chili powder, and cumin!

Ingredient: 1 tablespoon cooking oil, 1 medium onion finely chopped, 1/2 tsp. turmeric, 1 teaspoon ginger grated, 1 teaspoon mild red chili powder, 1 teaspoon cumin powder, 1 teaspoon salt, 3 cups whole brown lentils sprouted.

Optional Toppings: 1 plum tomato diced, 2 tablespoon cilantro chopped, 1 tablespoon fresh coconut grated, Egg cooked sunny side up, salt & pepper to taste.

Preparation: Turn Instant Pot to Sauté mode. Once the 'hot' sign displays, add oil. Add onions and cook for a minute. Cook covered with a glass lid on for another minute or until the onions become translucent stirring frequently. Add turmeric, ginger, red chili powder, salt and cumin powder. Mix well and add sprouted lentils. Add 1/3 cup of water and mix well. Close Instant Pot with the pressure valve to sealing. Cook on Manual for 1 min followed by Natural Pressure Release. Open Instant Pot, Garnish with tomatoes and cilantro. Add additional toppings - fresh grated coconut or eggs. Add salt and pepper to taste. Enjoy hot or cold.

Healthy Chocolate Instant Pot Steel Cut Oats: Satisfying & nourishing Healthy Chocolate Instant Pot Steel Cut Oats. Quick to make, simple & naturally sweetened with banana only. There is no added sugar at all! Just perfect for a hearty breakfast.

Ingredient: 1 cup / 176g / 6.2 oz. steel cut oats, 3 medium bananas, don't use large bananas as it will make the mixture too thick for the IP to handle, 3 tablespoons cocoa, 3½ cups / 840 mls / 28 FL oz. water, or use half non-dairy milk, half water.

Preparation: Add the oats, water and cocoa to the Instant Pot and stir well. Mash the bananas with a fork until a puree. A few small chunks are ok. Add them on top of the other ingredients and DO NOT stir. Put the lid on, make sure the steam vent is sealed and set to manual, high pressure, for 9 minutes. Then leave the pressure to release naturally. Once the pressure has been released and the pin has dropped, remove the lid and stir the oatmeal really well before serving. It will thicken up as it cools. You can add more water or milk before serving for a looser texture if you want.

Instant Pot Steel Cut Oats: Oatmeal is one of my favourite winter meals and Instant Pot Steel Cut Oats make it easier to have them every day. You can set them up the night before and wake up to a steaming hot bowl of oats. Plus you can make them sweet or savoury depending on how you choose to top them.

Ingredient: 1 1/2 cups water, 1/2 cup steel-cut oats.

Preparation: Add the water and oats to your Instant Pot. Put your lid on and make sure the vent is closed. Plug it in and select the manual setting and set to cook on high pressure for 3 minutes. The Instant Pot timer will begin counting down the time once it gets up to pressure. Allow the pressure to release naturally. You'll know when it's ready because the round silver pressure gauge will drop down. This will take about 5 to 10 minutes.

Homemade Instant Pot Almond Milk: While you do not need an Instant Pot to make a plant-based milk, this recipe does use one. It's the last minute plant based milk recipe that you'll have when you need it. (This is not raw almond milk.)

Ingredient: 2 cups water, 1 cup almonds, 4 cups water.

Preparation: Add the water and almonds to your Instant Pot and cook on high pressure for 10 minutes. Carefully manually release the pressure. Drain the almonds. Add the almonds and the 4 cups (946 ml) water to your blender and blend well. Strain through a nut milk bag and store in the refrigerator. The recipe makes an unsweetened plain non-dairy milk.

SOUPS, STEWS AND CURRIES BY INSTANT POT.

Thai Curried Butternut Squash Soup: Excited to have a warm bowl of creamy soupy goodness? This Thai Butternut Squash Soup made in the Instant Pot is what you have been waiting for. It is creamy, flavourful, healthy and vegan!

Ingredient: 1 tbsp. Oil, 1 cup Yellow Onion diced, 3 cloves Garlic minced, 1 tbsp. Ginger minced, 2 lbs. Butternut Squash peeled, seeded and cut into pieces, about 6 cups, 1 tbsp. Red curry paste adjust more to taste. 1.5 cups Vegetable broth, 1/2 can Coconut milk 14oz canned full fat, 1/2 tsp. Salt adjust to taste, Black Pepper add to taste (optional), 1/2 Lime juice, 2 tbsp. Roasted peanuts chopped, 2 tbsp. Coconut milk, 2 tbsp. Cilantro chopped, Red Chili flakes (optional)

Preparation: Start the instant pot in sauté mode and heat oil in it. Add diced onions, ginger and garlic and sauté for about 3 minutes. Add butternut squash, red curry paste, and broth and stir to combine. Press Cancel and close lid with vent in sealing position. Change the instant pot setting to manual or pressure cook mode at high pressure for 8 mins. After the instant pot beeps, let the pressure release naturally for 10 minutes then release the pressure manually. Use an immersion blender to blend the soup to a creamy texture. You can also transfer to a blender to blend the soup. Be careful while blending to avoid hot splatters. Add coconut milk, lime juice and stir well. Add salt, pepper and chili flakes to taste. Garnish the soup with cilantro, coconut milk and peanuts. Serve hot with a side of crusty bread!

Instant Pot Potato Soup: If you're looking for a delicious soup recipe for your Instant Pot, try this hearty and delicious Instant Pot Potato Soup. It comes together in just a few simple steps.

ingredient: 2 tbsp. olive oil, 3 leeks trimmed, thinly sliced, washed and drained, 1 lb. (450g) potatoes peeled and cubed, 4 cups (1 litre) vegetable stock hot, 0.5 tsp. ground nutmeg, Salt, Ground black pepper, 0.5 cups (125 ml) almond milk, or to taste.

Preparation: Press the sauté button on the Instant Pot. When the display reads Hot, add the oil. When hot add the leeks and sauté for about 5 mins till soft. Add the potatoes and cook for a couple of mins. Mix in the vegetable stock, nutmeg and seasoning. Put the lid on the Instant pot make sure the steam release part is pointing to sealing. Press the manual button and set the timer to 10 mins. Cook and once done release the pressure naturally over 10-15 mins. Add the almond milk and blend the soup into a puree using an immersion blender (or using a regular blender) Adjust seasoning and serve in bowls topped with toasted seeds or chilli oil.

Hearty Brown Lentil Soup: Hearty Brown Lentil & Vegetable Soup in the Instant Pot or Pressure Cooker. Make this warm soup on a cold & rainy (or snowy) day. Get cosy with this nutritious and easy to make vegan soup.

Ingredient: 1 cup Brown lentils (Whole Masoor Dal) rinsed, 2 tbsp. Olive Oil, 1 Onion small, diced (about 1 cup), 1 tbsp. Garlic minced, 2 Carrot cut into small pieces, 2 stalks Celery cut into small pieces, 3 cups Vegetable Broth or Water, 2 cups Baby Spinach packed, 1 tbsp. Lemon juice, 1/4 tsp. Sugar (optional), 1/2 tsp. Red Chili flakes (optional). 1 tsp. Ground Cumin, 1 tsp. Coriander powder, 1/2 tsp. Sumac (optional), 1/2 tsp. Ground Turmeric, 1 tsp. Salt, 1/2 tsp. Thyme dried (optional)

Preparation: Start the instant pot in SAUTE mode and heat oil in it. Add onions and garlic. Mix and sauté for 1 minute. Add carrots, celery and all spices along with thyme. Add the lentils and broth. Stir it all up. Press Cancel and close the lid with vent in sealing position. Set the instant pot to SOUP mode for 20 minutes. When the instant pot beeps, release the pressure naturally. Press Cancel. Add in spinach, lemon juice and sugar. Add some red chili flakes if you like. Stir it all up. Brown Lentil Soup is ready to enjoy!

Sweet Potato Kale Soup: Adding to my soup obsession, and wanting to make something special with my sweet potatoes, I created this lovely healthy soup that will be a friend to you, in the resolution keeping.

Ingredient: 2 Tbsp. Olive Oil, 1 small Onion, diced, 2 small Bay Leaves, 2 medium Sweet Potatoes, peeled and cubed (about 1 1/2 lbs.), 1/2 tsp. Coriander Powder, 1/2 tsp. Cumin, 1/8 tsp. Cinnamon, 1 tsp. Turmeric, 1 tsp. Kosher Salt (or 3/4 tsp. table salt), 1 3-4" sprig Fresh Rosemary (don't use dried), 3 cloves Garlic, pressed or minced, (1) 15 oz. can Diced Tomatoes, with juice, 1 tsp. Paprika, sweet, (1) 14 oz. can Coconut Milk (use light for fewer calories), 1 1/2 cups Water, 5 oz. Kale, chopped (1/2 of a 10 oz. bag).

Preparation: Turn on pressure cooker to the Sauté function. When the display reads "Hot" add the oil. Add the onion, and bay leaves. Cook, stirring occasionally, until onion starts to turn translucent. Add the sweet potatoes, coriander, cumin, cinnamon, turmeric, salt, rosemary, and garlic. Stir well and cook for about 1 minute. Add the tomatoes and paprika. Cook, stirring, for 2 minutes. Stir in the coconut milk, incorporating it well, and then add the water and stir well. Place the lid on the pressure cooker and lock in place. Turn the steam release knob to the Sealing position. Cancel the Sauté function and set to Pressure Cook (or Manual), and use the + or - button (or dial) to choose 5 minutes.

When cooking cycle has ended, let the pot sit undisturbed for 10 minutes (10 minutes of Natural Release). Then manually (Quick Release) the remaining steam by turning the steam release knob to the Venting position. When the pin in the lid drops down, open the lid carefully. Don't stir the soup yet. Add the kale to the soup and very gently fold it into the soup (Do this gently so the sweet potatoes don't all break up. You do want some of them to as this naturally thickens it. Use your own judgement on this). Let the soup sit for a couple of minutes so the kale can wilt. Then taste and adjust salt, if desired. Serve nice and hot. Garnish with some extra coconut milk, or heavy cream if you are not dairy-free. Enjoy!

Cream of Broccoli Soup: Enjoy this healthy Cream of Broccoli soup made in the Instant Pot (Pressure Cooker) in less than 30 minutes. This delicious comfort food can be enjoyed guilt free now, with this plant based vegan & gluten free recipe. Perfect for a quick satisfying lunch or dinner.

Ingredient: 1 tbsp. Oil, 1 cup Onion diced, 3 cloves Garlic minced, 1 lb Broccoli cut into small florets, about 5 cups, 1 cup Carrots cut into pieces, 1/3 cup Cashews, 2 cups Broth, 3/4 cup Coconut milk, 1 tbsp. Lemon juice (optional), Salt to taste, Black pepper to taste (optional). Basil (optional), 2 tbsp. Parsley chopped.

Preparation: Start the instant pot in sauté mode and heat oil in it. Add diced onions and garlic and sauté for about 3 minutes. Add broccoli, carrots, cashews and broth. Stir it all up. Press Cancel and close lid with vent in sealing position. Change the instant pot setting to manual or pressure cook mode at high pressure for 3 mins. After the instant pot beeps, let the pressure release naturally for 10 minutes then release the pressure manually. Add coconut milk.

Use an immersion blender to blend the soup to a creamy texture. You can also transfer to a blender to blend the soup. Be careful while blending to avoid hot splatters. Season the soup with salt, pepper and lemon juice. Top with parsley and basil to garnish. Enjoy with toasted bread!

Instant Pot Lasagna Soup: LASAGNA SOUP is totally a thing, you wouldn't believe how much savoury this dish can give you— unless, of course you try.

Ingredient: 32 oz. Rao's Marinara Sauce, 32 oz. Rao's Arrabbiata Sauce, 3 cups Mafalda Pasta or Campanile (Or broken Lasagne Noodles), 2 Serrano's, diced small, 4 garlic cloves, minced/grated, 3-4 Cups Spinach Leaves (fresh not frozen), 1 green bell pepper, diced small, 1 onion, diced small, 1/4 cup cilantro chopped, 1/4 cup parsley chopped, 1/4 cup scallions, sliced, 1/2 tsp. fresh oregano, finely minced, 4 cups Vegetable broth (I prefer Pacific Foods), 2 cups water, 1 cup parmesan cheese, 1 cup ricotta cheese, 1 cup mozzarella cheese, shredded, 1 Bay Leaf, 2 tbsp. oil.

Preparation: Set your IP to sauté mode and add two tablespoons of oil. Once the oil is hot, add the Serrano chillies and oregano and let splutter for a few moments. Add the onions and peppers and continue to cook for 3-4 minutes. Add garlic- stirring continuously so the garlic does not brown. Once the onions and peppers have softened a bit- add in the Rao's sauce, spinach, vegetable broth, 1 cup water, bay leaf, scallions, cilantro, and parsley. Stir well for a few minutes until all the ingredients are incorporated. Add in the pasta. Hit cancel on the IP and switch it to Pressure Cook on High Mode- for 3 minutes (If you use a different pasta than I did- just cut the cooking time on the box in half for the pressure cook time- my box said 6 minutes to al dente- so I cooked the pasta for 3 minutes). After 3 minutes- do a manual release (use a towel to protect your hands). Once the silver pin drops- open the IP.

The consistency should be soupy- if it is too thick- add water in one cup increments until you reach the desired consistency. If your pasta is undercooked- just set it on sauté mode and let it simmer until the pasta cooks. Add in the parmesan, mozzarella and ricotta. Add more or less cheese as you like- add salt per your taste (I did not add any salt in my recipe).

Vegan Instant Pot Cauliflower Soup: A healthy and healing Turmeric Cauliflower Soup made in the Instant Pot. This vegan & gluten free soup is so easy to make, and the result is creamy, satisfying goodness you will not want to stop eating!

Ingredient: 1 tbsp. Olive Oil, 3/4 cup Onion diced, 4 cloves Garlic minced, 1 head Cauliflower about 5 cups or 1.6lbs, cut into 2 inch florets, 1/2 cup Cashews, 1/2 tsp. Ground Turmeric, 1/2 tsp. Ground Cinnamon, 3 cups Vegetable broth, 1 tsp. Salt adjust to taste, 1 tbsp. Lemon juice, Parsley, Red Chili flakes (optional).

Preparation: Start the instant pot in sauté mode and heat oil in it. Add diced onions and garlic and sauté for about 3 minutes. Add cauliflower, cashews, turmeric, cinnamon, broth and salt. Stir it all up. Press Cancel and close lid with vent in sealing position. Change the instant pot setting to manual or pressure cook mode at high pressure for 3 mins. After the instant pot beeps, let the pressure release naturally for 10 minutes then release the pressure manually. Add the lemon juice. Use an immersion blender to blend the soup to a creamy texture. You can also transfer to a blender to blend the soup. Be careful while blending to avoid hot splatters. Top with parsley and some chili flakes (optional). Enjoy with toasted bread!

Instant Pot Vegetable Quinoa Soup: Ready for the easiest soup recipe of your life? You won't believe the flavours in this easy-to-make Instant Pot Vegetable Quinoa Soup!

Ingredient: 2 1/2 Tbsp. olive oil, 1Tbsp Italian seasoning, 1 cup chopped onion, 1 cup peeled and chopped carrots, 1 cup chopped celery, 6 cups low-sodium organic vegetable broth, 1 cup Quinoa, 1-1/2 cup tomatoes puree, Salt and freshly ground black pepper to taste, 1/2 cup chopped fresh green beans or Asparagus, 1 chopped zucchini, 3 cups baby spinach.

Preparation: Heat oil in pressure cooker set to Sauté on Normal. Cook onion, carrots, zucchini, asparagus, celery and baby spinach in hot oil and give it a quick stir. Add in the tomato puree, add the quinoa and vegetable stock, add Italian seasoning, salt, pepper to taste. Lock pressure cooker lid in place and set steam vent to Sealing. Select Soup/Stew and cook for 3 minutes on High pressure. Once the cooking cycle has completed, set steam vent to Venting to quick-release pressure. Stir the soup and season with salt and pepper to serve.

Minestrone Soup: A perfect soup that is a complete meal in itself – Beans, loads of veggies and pasta, topped with cheese and a side of bread. Vegetarian friendly and can easily be made gluten-free and vegan.

Ingredient: 2 tbsp. Olive Oil, 1 Onion diced, 1 tbsp. Garlic minced, 4 Tomato diced, 2 Celery Stalks chopped, 2 Carrot chopped, 1 Zucchini chopped, 1/2 cup Pasta (I used elbow macaroni), 32 oz. Vegetable Broth, 1 can White Kidney Beans 15oz (cannellini), 2 cups Spinach (Palak) chopped, 1/4 cup Parmesan cheese freshly grated (optional).

Preparation: Start the instant pot in SAUTE mode and heat olive oil in it. Add diced onions and minced garlic. Stir and sauté for 2 minutes. Add diced tomatoes and chopped celery, carrots and zucchini. Add in the Italian seasoning, salt, pepper and paprika. Add in the pasta, veggie broth and white kidney beans. Stir it all up. Make sure the pasta is under the broth. Press Cancel and set to SOUP setting (high pressure) for 20 minutes. (For firmer pasta, only cook for 10 minutes on SOUP setting) When the instant pot beeps, let the pressure release naturally for 5 minutes. Then manually release the pressure. If you have time, you can also allow a NPR. Stir in the chopped spinach and let it sit for 5 minutes. Garnish with parmesan cheese and minestrone soup is ready to serve.

Instant Pot Pumpkin Soup: This Instant Pot pumpkin soup is thick, creamy and perfectly seasoned with fall spices. Quick and easy to make, this soup recipe will fill you with warmth and comfort on those cold fall and winter days.

Ingredient: 4 tablespoons unsalted butter, 2 cups sweet onion chopped, 2 cloves garlic minced, 1 teaspoon ground cinnamon, ½ teaspoon ground nutmeg, ¼ teaspoon ground ginger, 4 cups unsalted vegetable stock, 2 tablespoons dark brown sugar, 1 teaspoon kosher salt or to taste, 1 can pumpkin puree 29 ounce, ½ cup heavy whipping cream.

preparation: Turn on the Instant Pot to 'Sauté' and using the 'Adjust' button, adjust the sauté heat level to 'Normal' and allow it to heat up for a few minutes so that the panel reads 'Hot' before adding the butter. Add the butter to the pot and, using a spoon or spatula, move it around the bottom of the hot liner to help it melt more quickly. Once the butter has melted and started to get hot, add the onion and cook, stirring occasionally until it becomes soft and translucent, 4 to 5 minutes. Do not allow the onions to brown. Add the garlic, stir into the onions and continue to sauté for another 1 to 2 minutes. Add the cinnamon, nutmeg, and ginger to the pot and mix them into the onions. Allow the spices to cook in the onions until they start to release their aroma, approximately 1 minute.

Turn off the 'Sauté' function and add the vegetable stock, brown sugar, and salt then mix everything together well. Add the pumpkin puree, just spooning it into the centre of the pot. Do not mix it into the stock. Close the pot and set the pressure release valve to 'Sealing'. Select the 'Soup' function and set the cook time to 10 minutes. Once the 10 minute cook time has completed, perform a 5 minute NPR (natural pressure release). As soon as all of the pressure has been released, open the Instant Pot. Turn off the Instant Pot and allow the soup to cool for a few minutes. Using an immersion blender, puree all of the ingredients and then mix in the heavy whipping cream.

Serve and enjoy!

Instant Pot Creamy Tomato Soup: Instant Pot Creamy Tomato Soup is delicious and nutritious with lots of veggies. Made with fresh tomatoes along with carrots, celery, onion and a hint of garlic, topped with some cream and cheese. Oh so creamy...you will love it!

Ingredient: 1 tbsp. Butter or Oil, 7 cloves Garlic, 1/2 Onion chopped, 5 Carrot chopped (I used small thin carrots), 3 stalks Celery chopped, 5 Tomato chopped, 3/4 cup Broth or water, 1/4 cup Romano Cheese grated (optional), 1/4 cup Cream heavy whipping, use coconut milk for vegan, 2 tbsp. Cilantro to garnish, Salt & Pepper to taste.

Preparation: Start the instant pot in Sauté mode and wait till it displays HOT. Add butter and let it melt. Add chopped onions, garlic and cook for a minute. Add in carrots and celery to instant pot. Add in the chopped tomatoes. Add broth to instant pot and stir it with all the veggies making sure nothing is stuck to the bottom of the pot. Press cancel and close the lid with vent in sealing position. Start instant pot in manual or pressure cook mode at high pressure for 6 minutes. When the instant pot beeps, let the pressure release naturally.

Open the lid and use an immersion blender to puree the mixture until it is smooth. Or transfer to a blender and carefully blend the soup in batches. (If you like your tomato soup to be very smooth, you can strain it over a fine mesh strainer) Stir in the cream and cheese. Simmer for another 2 minutes on sauté mode until the cheese mixes well. Add salt and pepper to taste. Give the soup a taste and adjust broth or seasoning to taste, adding any extra of whatever you prefer to get your ideal thickness and flavour. Garnish with cilantro and grated cheese (optional). Creamy Tomato Soup is ready to be served with garlic bread or your favourite side.

Tuscan Vegetable Soup: Tuscan Vegetable Soup Instant Pot Recipe is an easy + delicious + nutritious recipe. It is loaded with seasonal vegetables and cannellini beans and mildly flavoured with seasonings. The soup is light in calories but very filling. Add some shell pasta in it or put some bread on the side and make it a complete meal.

Ingredient: 1 Tbsp. Olive Oil, 3 Cloves Garlic chopped fine, 1 Medium Onion, red or white cut into chunky pieces, 2 Large Tomatoes cut into chunky pieces, 4 Sticks Celery cut into chunky pieces, 1 Medium Zucchini cut into chunky pieces, 1 Large Carrot cut into chunky pieces, 1 Cup Spinach, 1 Can Cannellini Beans drained, 2 Tbsp. Tomato Paste, 1 Tsp. Rosemary, dry, To Taste Salt and Black Pepper, 5 Cups Water, 1/2 Tsp. Cayenne Pepper or Fancy Paprika this is optional but elevates the taste to another level.

Preparation: Set the instant pot to sauté mode on MORE. When it displays HOT, add olive oil to it. After 30 seconds, add onions and garlic to the hot oil. Sauté for 2 minutes till onions become soft. Now add celery and carrots to the pot. Cook for 1 minute and then add cannellini beans + all the remaining vegetables + tomato paste + seasonings + herbs to the pot. Give it a good stir. Add 5 cups of water. Stir again. Place the lid and Switch off the sauté mode. Place the floating vent to CLOSE. Set the SOUP / BROTH MODE to NORMAL for 6 minutes. After the cooking is done and you hear the beep. There are 2 things you can do- 1). Release the pressure immediately and serve the soup while warm. IT is fully cooked and does not need Natural Pressure Release for further cooking. OR 2). If you are making it in the morning and coming back in the evening for a hearty soup, then, do not worry about releasing the pressure. Little over cooking will make vegetables slightly soft that's it but will still taste awesome.

Easy Jackfruit Curry: Young green Jackfruit makes a great shredded meat sub. Easy, Vegan, Soy-free Gluten-free Grain-free Indian curry. Simple spices, amazing flavour.

Ingredient: 1 tsp. oil, 1/2 tsp. (0.5 tsp.) cumin seeds, 1/2 tsp. (0.5 tsp.) mustard seeds, 1/2 tsp. (0.5 tsp.) nigella seeds, 2 bay leaves, 2 dried red chilies, 1 small onion chopped, 5 cloves of garlic chopped, 1 inch ginger chopped, 1 tsp. coriander powder, 1/2 tsp. (0.5 tsp.) turmeric, 1/4 tsp. (0.25 tsp.) black pepper, 2 medium tomatoes pureed or 1.5 cups puree, 20 oz. (566 g) can green Jackfruit, drained, rinsed and squeezed to remove excess brine. Also chop into smaller pieces if too big. 1/2 to 3/4 tsp. salt or to taste, 1 to 1.5 cups (235 to 353 ml) water.

Preparation: Heat oil in a skillet over medium heat. When hot, add cumin, mustard and nigella seeds and let them start to sizzle or pop. 1 minute. Add bay leaves and red chilies and cook for a few seconds. Add in the onion, garlic and ginger and a pinch of salt. Cook until translucent. 5 to 6 minutes. Stir occasionally. Add coriander, turmeric, black pepper and mix well. Add pureed tomato, salt and Jackfruit. Mix. Cover and cook for 15 minutes. Add tomato puree and cook for 2 minutes, then add jackfruit, salt and 1/2 to 1 cup water. Close the lid and pressure cook for 7 to 8 minutes once the cooker comes to pressure (manual 8 mins on IP). Wait for natural release.

DESSERT RECIPES.

New York-Style Instant Pot Cheesecake: The cheesecake is an ideal make-ahead dessert—it's better after a rest in the fridge and will knock your dinner guests' socks off. Plus, since the decadent dessert comes together rather effortlessly in the Instant Pot, there's no reason not to make one. Serve with classic cherries or strawberries, or drizzle with chocolate or caramel (or both!).

Ingredient: 3 tablespoons sugar, 5 tablespoons butter, 9 large graham crackers, pulsed into crumbs, 2 tablespoons ground pecans, 1/4 teaspoon cinnamon, 12 ounces cream cheese (or 1 1/2 packages), 1/4 teaspoon kosher salt, 2 teaspoons lemon zest, 2 teaspoons vanilla extract, 1 tablespoon cornstarch, 1/2 cup + 2 tablespoons granulated sugar, 2 large eggs + 1 egg yolk, 1/2 cup sour cream.

Preparation: Position a rack in the centre of the oven and preheat the oven to 350ºF if you plan on baking the crust. If you're freezing it, you can skip this step. Regardless of which method you use, wrap your 6 or 7-inch spring form pan tightly in foil and spray the inside of the pan with non-stick cooking spray.

CRUST: combine the butter and sugar in a microwave-safe bowl and zap until the butter melts, about 30-40 seconds. In a medium bowl, combine the cracker crumbs, pecans, and cinnamon. Pour the melted butter on top and using a rubber spatula mix until the crumbs are covered in the butter. Press the crumb mixture into the bottom of the prepared pan and about 1-inch up the sides. Place the pan in the freezer for 15-20 minutes or bake for 10 minutes. If baking, allow the crust to cool to room temperature before proceeding.

CHEESECAKE FILLING: In the bowl of a stand mixer fitted with the paddle attachment, beat the cream cheese, salt, vanilla, lemon zest, and corn-starch until smooth, about 1-2 minutes. Add the sugar and let it mix in completely before adding the eggs one at a time. Add the sour cream and mix until just combined. Pour the batter into the crust. Cover the top of the spring form pan with a piece of foil and wrap it tightly around the rim.

PRESSURE COOK: Pour 1 1/4 cups of water into the base of the instant pot and place the steaming rack on the bottom. Place the spring form pan on the rack. Lock the lid in place and seal the vent. Cook the cheesecake on manual high pressure for 37 minutes and allow the Instant Pot to naturally release its pressure for 25 minutes afterward (the 'keep warm' setting should still be on, you don't want to turn your IP off completely).

LET COOL: carefully remove the spring form pan from the IP then remove the foil. Using a piece of kitchen towel, gently wipe the surface of the cheesecake if there is any moisture on the surface of the cake. Allow the cheesecake to cool to room temperature, about 3 hours before placing it in the refrigerator to cool overnight. Cheesecake can be prepared 24-48 hours in advance. Top with whipped cream, berries, or apple or cherry pie filling before serving!

Instant Pot Banana Bread: This pressure cooker banana bread is a moist, dense bread, so making it in the instant Pot is perfect!

Ingredient: 3 Ripe Bananas, mashed, 1/2 cup Butter, softened, 1/2 cup Brown Sugar, 1/2 cup White Sugar, 2 Eggs, beaten, 1 tsp. Vanilla, 1/4 cup Buttermilk (or Sour Cream), 2 cups All Purpose Flour, sifted, 1 tsp. Baking Soda, 1 tsp. Baking Powder, 1/4 tsp. Cinnamon, 1/2 tsp. Salt, 6 qtr. or 8 qtr. Electric Pressure Cooker, Trivet with handles, Mixing Bowls, Hand Mixer

6 cup Bundt or Cake Pan (7" is ideal), Baking Spray, Foil.

Preparation: Add 1 1/2 cups of water to the inner liner of the pressure cooker (2 cups if using the 8 qtr.). Spray the cake pan with baking spray and set aside. In a mixing bowl, mash the ripe bananas using a fork. In another mixing bowl, use a hand mixer to cream the butter and sugars together. Add the beaten eggs and vanilla to the creamed butter/sugar mixture. Use a spoon to mix well. Stir the bananas and sour cream/buttermilk into the butter/sugar mixture and mix well. In another mixing bowl, sift together the flour, baking soda, baking powder, cinnamon and salt. Add the dry ingredients to the wet ingredients and gently stir by hand, until just moistened. Spoon the batter into prepared cake/Bundt pan and cover with foil, leaving some room for the bread to rise a little. Gently crimp the edges. Set the trivet on the counter, and put the cake/Bundt pan on it. Carefully place it in the pot using the handles. Close the lid and set the steam release knob to the Sealing position. Press the Pressure Cook/Manual button or dial, then the +/- button or dial to select 50 minutes for a Bundt style pan, and 55 minutes for a regular 7" pan. High pressure.

After the cook time is finished, let the pot sit undisturbed for 15 minutes (15 minute natural release). Then turn the steam release knob to the Venting position to release the remaining steam/pressure. After all of the pressure is out and the pin in the lid drops down, open it and use silicone mitts or pot holders to very carefully remove the cake/bundt pan from the pressure cooker, using the trivet handles. Carefully remove the foil, and let the banana bread sit for 10-15 minutes to cool a bit. Then release the bread from the pan onto a plate. Either invert the pan, or with a push pan, set it on a can and gently push the pan down.

Serve the banana bread warm, slathered in butter, or let it cool and drizzle with my Vanilla Icing Glaze.

Pressure Cooker Applesauce: You'll love how quickly and easily you can make applesauce in a pressure cooker. It truly takes mere minutes to cook and yields delicious tender-yet-chunky results. Use a combination of tart and sweet apples, or adjust the amounts of brown sugar and lemon juice in this applesauce recipe to achieve the perfect sweet-sour flavour.

Ingredient: 2 1/2 pounds apples, 1/4 cup brown sugar, 1 teaspoon cinnamon, 3/4 cups apple juice (or apple cider), 1 tablespoon lemon juice, Pinch salt.

Preparation: Peel and core the apples and cut them into equally sized wedges. In a pressure cooker, combine the apples, brown sugar, cinnamon, apple juice or cider, lemon juice, and salt. Cover the cooker and lock it into place, then place the cooker on the stove over high heat. Bring the pressure cooker up to high pressure, then immediately start the timer for 4 minutes and reduce the heat to maintain pressure.

After 4 minutes, remove the pressure cooker from the heat and release pressure using the natural method (in other words, just let the closed pressure cooker rest until the pressure gauge indicates the steam pressure has been released, about 10 minutes). Carefully open lid, angling it away from you to avoid getting burned by the steam. With a wooden spoon, stir the apples, breaking them up large chunks, until you've achieved the desired consistency. If you like a very smooth applesauce, you can put the mixture in a food processor and pulse it a few times, or put it through a food mill.

Instant Pot Arroz Con Leche: Arroz con Leche is a traditional Hispanic rice pudding that's sweet, rich, and creamy and served with a dash of cinnamon. A warm bowl of this dessert is guaranteed to comfort your soul and satisfy your sweet tooth.

Ingredient: 1 cup long grain rice white, I use the rice measuring cup provided with the Instant Pot, 1 ¼ cups water, 2 cups whole milk, ⅛ teaspoon kosher salt, 1 can sweetened condensed milk 14 oz., 1 teaspoon vanilla extract, ground cinnamon.

Preparation: Rinse the rice using a mesh strainer until the water runs clean. I like the brand Mahatma. Add the milk, water, rice and salt to the Instant Pot and stir. Set the Instant Pot on the Porridge setting (20 minutes). Allow for a 10 minute NPR (natural pressure release) and then release the remaining pressure and open the pot. Add the can of condensed milk and the teaspoon of vanilla extract to the rice. Mix it all together.

Serve warm and enjoy!

Pressure Cooker Chocolate Pots De Crème: Chocolate Pots de Crème is a decadent and creamy chocolate custard dessert. Baked chocolate custard made in an Instant Pot is effortless and quick. This Pressure Cooker Chocolate Pots de Crème recipe is elegant enough for entertaining, but simple enough for a casual weeknight dessert.

Ingredient: 1 1/2 cups heavy cream, 1/2 cup whole milk, 5 large egg yolks, 1/4 cup sugar, pinch of salt, 8 ounces bittersweet chocolate, melted, whipped cream and grated chocolate for decoration, optional.

Preparation: In a small saucepan, bring the cream and milk to a simmer. In a large mixing bowl, whisk together egg yolks, sugar, and salt. Slowly whisk in the hot cream and milk. Whisk in chocolate until blended. Pour into 6 custard cups. (I used 1/2 pint mason jars.) Add 1 1/2 cups of water to the pressure cooker and place the trivet in the bottom. Place 3 cups on the trivet and place a second trivet on top of the cups. Stack the remaining three cups on top of the second trivet. Lock the lid in place. Select High Pressure and set the timer for 6 minutes. When beep sounds, turn off pressure cooker and use a natural pressure release for 15 minutes and then do a quick pressure release to release any remaining pressure. When valve drops carefully remove lid.

Carefully remove the cups to a wire rack to cool uncovered. When cool, refrigerate covered with plastic wrap for at least 4 hours or overnight.

2-ingredient Cheesecake (Instant Pot Indian Cheesecake): You only need two ingredients to make this Instant Pot Cheesecake.

Ingredient: 1 (14 ounce) can condensed milk (sweetened), 1 cup whole milk yogurt (full-fat yogurt or full-fat Greek yogurt), Oil or butter, for greasing ramekins or cheesecake pan.

Preparation: Add the condensed milk and yogurt to a bowl and mix well. Pour this mixture into 4 (6 ounce) greased ramekins or into a cheesecake pan and cover the pan(s) with foil.

Add 2 cups water into the steel inner pot, then place the trivet/wire rack that came with your pressure cooker into the pot. Place the ramekins or the cheesecake pan on top of the rack. Secure the lid, close the pressure valve and cook for 25 minutes at high pressure if using ramekins or 30 minutes at high pressure if using a cheesecake pan. Naturally release pressure for 20 minutes, then release any remaining pressure (do not leave the cheesecake sitting in the pot). The cheesecake should be set (it shouldn't wiggle). Stick a toothpick into the cheesecake and if it comes out clean, it's done. Allow the cheesecakes to cool down on a wire rack. I find it easiest to unmould the cheesecake while slightly warm. (To unmould the cheesecake from ramekins, use a paring knife to loosen the sides of the cake from the ramekin if needed and then flip it out onto a plate. To unmould the cheesecake from a cheesecake pan, use a paring knife to loosen the sides of the cake from the pan — then I suggest watching this video to get a better idea of how I remove the cake).

Put the cheesecake in the fridge to chill for 4-6 hours.

Instant Pot Vegan Borscht: It's very easy to make: Just cut and prepare the veggies, put them into the pot, and start the Soup program.

ingredient: 1 tablespoon canola oil, or as needed1/2 large onion, diced8 cups water, divided1/2 medium head cabbage, finely shredded3/4 pound beets, grated1/2 pound potatoes, cut into small cubes2 carrots, grated1 green bell pepper, chopped (optional)3 bay leaves-salt and ground black pepper to taste.

Preparation: Turn on a multi-functional pressure cooker (such as Instant Pot(R)) and select sauté function. Add oil and onion. Cook, stirring often, until translucent, 3 to 5 minutes. Add a splash of water to stop cooking. Add 8 cups water, cabbage, beets, potatoes, carrots, bell pepper, bay leaves, salt, and pepper to the pot. Close and lock the lid. Select high pressure according to manufacturer's instructions; set timer for 40 minutes. Allow 10 to 15 minutes for pressure to build. Release pressure carefully using the quick-release method according to manufacturer's instructions, about 5 minutes. Unlock and remove the lid.

Instant Pot Vegan Apple Cake: Easy Instant Pot vegan apple cake is so moist and delicious, this cake is vegan gluten-free, oil-free. This flavourful apple crumb cake is loaded with fresh apples and a hint of spice. Serve it as a snack, breakfast cake, or dessert.

Ingredient: 1 medium apple, peeled and finely cubed, 1 medium ripe banana, peeled and mashed, 2 tablespoons almond flour, 1 tablespoon sugar, 1/4 teaspoon cinnamon, 1 cup almond milk, 2 tablespoons ground flaxseeds, 2 teaspoons vanilla, 1 cup brown rice flour, 1/2 cup rolled oats, 1/2 cup almond flour, 3/4 cup sugar, 1 tablespoon baking powder, 1/2 teaspoon cinnamon

1/4 teaspoon nutmeg, 1/4 teaspoon salt.

Preparation: Line the 6-inch cake pan with parchment paper and spray or lightly brush with oil and set aside. To prepare crumb topping mix almond meal or flour, sugar, and cinnamon in a bowl and set aside. In a medium bowl mix the almond milk, ground flaxseeds, banana, and vanilla. Set aside In a large bowl, add brown rice flour, rolled oats, almond flour, sugar, ground flaxseed, baking powder, cinnamon, nutmeg, and sea salt. Add the almond milk mixture and stir to combine. Fold in mashed banana and apple pieces. Scoop batter in cake pan. Sprinkle crumb topping mix on top of the batter. Cover the pan with the lid or foil if using another 6-inch cake pan. Place the covered container with your cake batter on the trivet. Lower the trivet in the inner pot of the Instant Pot using the sling handle. Seal the Instant Pot on Manual High Pressure for 50 minutes, when cooking is complete Natural Pressure Release for 10 minutes after complete then turn the knob to venting to release the remaining steam. Open the lid, and carefully remove the baking pan using the sling handle.

Allow the cake to cool in the pan for 10 minutes then gently remove the cake from the pan onto a cooling rack to completely cool. Delicious topped with vegan vanilla ice cream or coconut whipped cream, or served as a breakfast cake.

Instant Pot Apple Crisp: This Instant Pot apple crisp made with organic granola is quick and delicious! It's a cosy vegan dessert recipe that cooks in minutes in a pressure cooker.

Ingredient: 1 1/2 cups One Degree Organic Sprouted Oat Vanilla Chia Granola, 1/4 cup coconut oil, 1/4 cup organic brown sugar, 4 large or 6 small tart apples (like Granny Smith), enough for 5 cups sliced, 2 tablespoons maple syrup, 1 teaspoon cinnamon, plus 1/8 teaspoon for serving, 1/2 teaspoon ground ginger, 1 teaspoon vanilla extract, 2/3 cup water, Zest of 1/2 lemon, for serving.

Preparation: In a small bowl, mix together the granola, room temperature coconut oil and 2 tablespoons brown sugar; you may need to use your hands to bring everything together. (Note: The granola we used was lightly sweet. If using a very sweet granola, you can lessen the sugar in the topping.) Peel and slice the apples into about 1/4 slices, enough for 5 cups, and place them in the bowl of the Instant Pot. Stir in 2 tablespoons brown sugar, then the maple, cinnamon, ginger, vanilla and water. Smooth the apples into an even layer and pour the granola mixture over the top, covering the apples. Lock the top of the Instant Pot. Pressure cook on high for 2 minutes. (Note: It takes about 5 minutes for the pot to "preheat" before it starts cooking. During cooking, avoid touching the metal part of the lid.) After the pot beeps, immediately do a Quick Release: vent the remaining steam by moving the pressure release handle to "Venting", covering your hand with a towel or hot pad. (Never put your hands or face near the steam release valve when releasing steam.)

While the crisp is cooking, prepare the garnish: Zest 1 lemon. Mix it together with 1/4 teaspoon cinnamon. After the Quick Release, remove the lid. Turn off the pot and let the crisp sit uncovered for 5 minutes (make sure Keep Warm feature is turned off). This lets the sauce thicken; the oats will be intentionally chewy, not crunchy. Scoop the crisp into bowls and add a pinch of the lemon zest garnish. If desired, serve with vegan vanilla ice cream or Coconut Whipped Cream.

SUMMARY.

I am certain that you have enjoyed most, if not all of our instant pot recipes as they are some of the finest dishes across the continents. We are committed to making your vegan journey an absolute treat and would welcome any inquiries that you may have; we'd be glad to give our suggestions.

www.ingramcontent.com/pod-product-compliance
Lightning Source LLC
Chambersburg PA
CBHW071843080526
44589CB00012B/1093